W9-AQB-930

PRAISE FOR
WHAT'S YOUR STORY?

"This is a smart book, an important book and a book you need to read. If your message isn't getting through, here's why."
— SETH GODIN, author, *All Marketers Are Liars*

"Storytelling is becoming more and more recognized as a critical element of great leadership. Craig is at the leading edge of this very important trend. The book not only provides the context of why storytelling is so important but, more important, provides the tools to help anyone put storytelling into practice today."
—BRIAN J. MCNAMARA, Senior Vice President/NA Region Head, Novartis OTC

"A great reminder that all businesses are 'people businesses.' In today's fast-paced techno-world, it's easy to get caught in rapid responses vs. relationship building. If you want people to remember you, slow down and read this book."
—BOB TORKELSON, President and COO, Trinchero Family Estates

"The story is the most powerful tool of the effective communicator, and in this book you'll learn more than you ever imagined about effectively using stories. Craig Wortmann delivers in a book that is chock full of insights and great ideas."
—MARK SANBORN, Author of *The Fred Factor* and *You Don't Need a Title to Be a Leader*

"This is a very valuable book on the power of telling stories to create personal and organizational change. I highly recommend it."
—JACK CANFIELD, Coauthor, *Chicken Soup for the Soul*® series and *The Success Priniciples*™

In *What's Your Story? Using Stories to Ignite Performance and Be More Successful*, author, entrepreneur, and master storyteller Craig Wortmann demonstrates the powerful impact stories have on the three most common performance challenges—leadership, strategic selling, and motivation.

While the technique of telling stories is the oldest form of communication—it's also the one form that rises above the din of our information-saturated environment and delivers messages in a way that connects with people, bringing ideas to life and making them actionable and memorable.

Leaders at all levels learn how to use the toolset developed in this book—the Win Book, Story Matrix, and Story Coach—to capture and tell the right stories at the right time to inspire their own performance and the performance of the those around them. Through real-life scenarios, illustrations, quotations, tools, and examples, Wortmann guides you through the process of uncovering your stories.

CRAIG
WORTMANN

WHAT'S YOUR STORY?

USING STORIES TO IGNITE
PERFORMANCE AND BE
MORE SUCCESSFUL

SALESENGINE

This publication is designed to provide accurate and authoritative information in regard to the subject matter covered. It is sold with the understanding that the publisher is not engaged in rendering legal, accounting, or other professional service. If legal advice or other expert assistance is required, the services of a competent professional should be sought.

First Edition: 2006
Published by Kaplan Publishing, a division of Kaplan, Inc.
Typesetter and Cover Designer: Renata Graw

Library of Congress Cataloging-in-Publication Data

Wortmann, Craig.
　　What's your story? : using stories to ignite performance and be more successful/Craig Wortmann.
　　　　p. cm.
　　Includes bibliographical references and index.
　　ISBN-13: 978-1-4195-3556-7
　　ISBN-10: 1-4195-3556-0
1. Communication organizations.　　2. Storytelling.　　3. Leadership.　　I. Title.
　　HD30.3.W67 2006
　　658.4'5--dc22

2006015549

06 07 08 10 9 8 7 6 5 4 3 2 1

Second Edition: 2012
Published by Sales Engine, Evanston, IL
Type and Graphics Editing: Wendy Ruel, IPM Group, Inc., Overland Park, KS

　ISBN-13: 978-0-9853253-0-5

© 2006, 2012 by Craig Wortmann

All rights reserved. The text of this publication, or any part thereof, may not be reproduced in any manner whatsoever without written permission from the publisher.

Printed in the United States of America

This book is available at special quantity discounts to use for sales promotions, employee premiums, or educational purposes. For more information, contact info@salesengine.com or Sales Engine, 1555 Sherman Avenue Suite 220, Evanston, Illinois 60201

Craig Wortmann is an entrepreneur and three-time CEO who speaks to and motivates audiences all over the world on the topics of Entrepreneurship & Sales, Storytelling and Leadership. He motivates, inspires and delights on these topics bringing them to life through the powerful stories he tells. Craig transfers his knowledge through coaching and the application of tools he has developed that underlie high performance and drive success for leaders in each of these areas.

Craig is the Founder and CEO of Sales Engine, a firm that helps companies build and tune their sales engine. Previously, Craig was recruited to join start-up WisdomTools as CEO, which he ran, grew and then successfully sold to a larger firm. And then he did it again. As the CEO of ClearGauge, an interactive marketing and web strategy firm, Craig executed a turnaround and high-valuation sale by building the sales engine, developing a new web presence, and cutting costs.

Craig is a clinical professor at the University of Chicago Booth School of Business, where he teaches Building the New Venture and Entrepreneurial Selling, an Inc. Magazine Award-Winning "Top Ten" course. Craig also designed and teaches a course called Personal Leadership Insights that looks at the knowledge, skills and discipline that serve as a foundation for developing one's own leadership capital.

Craig lives in Evanston with his wife, two children and their dog, Mr Chips.

DEDICATION

To my parents, Jeanine and Donald Wortmann. Mom, your love and persistent coaching helped my find my own voice. And Dad, you are simply the greatest man I've ever known.

If, in the final analysis, I have been one-tenth the parent that each of you has been, I will have succeeded.

ACKNOWLEDGMENTS

My wife, Jill Wortmann, is the reason this book exists. Jill, you encouraged me to get these ideas out there, and you helped to drive this effort from start to finish. Thank you so much for your support, your help in thinking things through, your time spent reading draft after draft, your incisive editing, and most of all for your belief.

I also want to thank two other smart and talented women who bravely read the first draft: my friends Lisa Schumacher and Kara Cardinale. As first drafts go, this thing was really scary. But you persevered, and your suggestions were invaluable. This book is clearer, tighter, and just a lot better thanks to you two.

Between being a dad and husband, writing this book, and running a small company, my schedule was a little nuts for the better part of a year. And there was very little time for fun diversions. So, I also want to thank a very special group of guys, all from one extended family—the Skalinders and Anichs. Gents, thank you sincerely for letting me, a nonrelative, join your 'BNO' team, and for giving me a much-needed break right in the middle of an otherwise hectic week.

Many thanks to the incredible team at Kaplan Publishing. Thanks to you all, this experience has been an incredible learning journey for me. Thank you so much for your patience, your support, your powerful ideas, and your enthusiasm. You all went way above and beyond for me at every step. Every author should be so lucky. Eileen Johnson, this was, after all, YOUR idea! You shouldn't have asked me that fateful question over coffee: "Craig, so you talk about stories a lot... what does that mean?" And Michael Cunningham, your ideas and comments on writing and structure are all over this effort. Thanks for the education you have given me. Michael Shelley, thanks to you for getting the ball rolling by truly understanding the power of stories and WisdomTools. Roy Lipner, you have one helluva team my friend. Thanks for letting me be a part of it.

The illustrations and graphics that you will find here are the work of a very talented designer, Renata Graw. Renata, thank you for taking my chicken-scratch drawings and making them come alive. Your sense of clean but powerful design is inspirational.

And to all of the energetic, talented people of WisdomTools, past and present. They say that a good wine takes time to "cure," and that it acquires its flavor in each step of the process, from the soil to the sunlight to the aging. WisdomTools is inventing an entirely new way to help organizations be more effective, and each of you added your own flavor to our company. Thank you for helping us build great stories and deliver client delight.

I wrote this book because I wanted to help people, to learn how to write, and to tell my stories in a different way. So I want to acknowledge you, the reader, for joining me in this journey.

CONTENTS

A RUSHING RIVER

This book is written for people who want to make a difference; people who want to build, create, learn, share, and inspire; people who want to give themselves and others the powerful gift of story.

What *is* your story? Have you thought about it? Certainly, you are full of stories. We all are. Stories are one of the things that make life and work fun and fulfilling. They are all around us every day as we move through the to-dos, experiences, ups and downs, and all of the other "stuff" of life.

Imagine for a moment that you are standing knee-deep in the middle of a rushing river. The water flows past you, and underneath your feet are rocks and sediment. You are holding a dented metal pan with a screen on the bottom, and you reach down into the riverbed and pull up a panful. As you shake the mud and grit out of the pan, gold appears. Gold nuggets. These gold nuggets represent the experiences—the stories—of your life. The mud and grit that get shaken back into the river represent all of the forgettable data and details of your life—the stuff that happens in between the stories and experiences.

Now imagine yourself getting off of the elevator at work and walking into a meeting. You are in the midst of a rushing river of information. You have e-mails to attend to, voicemails, presentations, and paperwork. You have responsibilities and goals and a limited amount of time. Empowered by technology, information comes at you nearly 24/7 from many different angles. Your "pan" fills very quickly. In fact, your pan may fill so quickly that you often find yourself just trying to stay ahead of the mud and grit without ever getting to touch the gold!

But it is in experiencing and telling these stories—the gold nuggets—that we establish a connection to each other and to the organization. The gold is the stuff that allows leaders to lead and people to perform. All of the rest is just "mud and grit."

INFORMATION REVOLUTION

Over the past couple of decades, technology has transformed our organizations and our work lives. We now have access to more information than we could ever hope to use. Indeed, information is now, quite literally, "in the air."

Technology has helped us capture most of the high-value information in our organizations. Thanks to technology, we now know who our most profitable customers are, how they behave, what they purchase, and how much they spend. We know how our entire supply chain is affected by a change in pricing strategy and we know how to distribute trucks or call volumes across our different resources. We can give our people access to their benefits information through an employee portal, their training through a learning management system, their customer information through customer relationship management (CRM), and the company's resources through enterprise resource management (ERM). That is an incredible amount of information that has now been parsed, categorized, tagged, and made available to leaders and employees.

Unfortunately, we haven't captured the highest value information of all, the stories that hold all of the people and tools and technologies together. Stories about what's expected of people in this organization. Stories about how we succeed and how we fail, what's important and what's not, how to get things done, how to manage, how to sell, and how to lead. We haven't captured stories that show people how to make ethical decisions, how to delight customers, how to streamline operations, and how to balance work and life. But these are the stories that hold all of our systems together. In fact, these stories are the glue that holds the whole organization together, just as stories of our history, our parents, and our friends hold families and communities together. These are the stories that become the fabric of large organizations and the grit that helps entrepreneurial companies succeed in the face of overwhelming odds. These are the stories that need to be told—the gold that should be passed around.

The truth is that we don't have a "system" to hold this most valuable information. And if there is no system, it doesn't get captured. This book is a kind of "system." Its purpose is to show you how to capture the high-value information that is all around you—the gold—and put it to use to impact your own performance and the performance of the organization. *This book will show you why stories are powerful and how to capture, organize, and tell those stories in a way that inspires your performance and the performance of those around you.*

Lest I be accused of being a Luddite, I think that most technology is extremely beneficial. As leaders, we have a plethora of tools to use in our communications. We have more ways than ever to reach out to people and build relationships, and we must make daily choices with our communications. But we must be conscious and *intentional* about how we use these tools.

E-mail, PowerPoint slides, pagers, and phones are the most common ways we communicate. In the crush of the average day, we make many snap decisions about our communications, often unconsciously. But what happens to the content of the message? As media analyst and philosopher Marshall McLuhan pointed out, too often the message gets shaped by the medium, so leaders strip away the extraneous material and give us the bullet points; just what we need to know—delivered fast. Most communications end up as disembodied information that is out of context, and, as such, doesn't connect with people. This means that we end up filling people's pans with more mud and grit and detail instead of offering them a gold nugget that will be much more valuable to them.

Stories bring information to life by making it actionable, memorable, and lifelike. Stories bring back the context, color, feeling, and meaning of our work. By showing people how to have success and where the pitfalls are, stories help people understand what it feels like to be "in the situation," and they learn by the examples of others'

"Learning is like Velcro. An unfiltered fact is not a complete fastener. Only one side of learning is made up of facts; the other consists of stories—that is, ideas and images."

– RICHARD SAUL WURMAN[1]

decisions. Adding stories makes communications "stickier"—the degree to which our communications are memorable and actionable.

In my work with leaders and stories over the past ten years, I have found that leaders are hungry for a different way to engage their people. I have also found that a leader's own stories of success and failure are the most potent for improving performance. *It is the leader's ability to translate his or her experiences into stories that gives that leader a performance advantage.*

NATURAL RESOURCES

Stories combine two elements that make them truly powerful tools: utility and significance. Many of the tools that we currently use in organizations have one or the other, but not both. From our cell phones to our CRM systems, our technology tools have tremendous utility. They are packed with features; the Swiss Army knives of our time. But they lack significance—a connection to what we as human beings care about, what builds relationships and motivates us to perform better.

The tools in our organizations that do connect with what we care about, the tools that we use to enhance performance and motivate people, have significance but limited utility. The pay packages and incentive systems, benefits, vacation policies, training conferences, and awards dinners that help us show up and perform, don't "scale." They often are one-use-only tools whose effect is felt and then dissipates quickly.

Stories don't dissipate. They hold their utility and significance long after the originator of the story is gone. Anyone who has worked for a large organization like the Red Cross or IBM, or even an entrepreneurial business that has some staying power, knows that some stories never die. The legends have utility long after their namesakes have disappeared.

Unlike other tools, techniques, consulting services, and systems that we have to purchase, stories are natural resources. They lie just under the surface of any organization, like an aquifer. Just as countries tap into their natural resources in order to create wealth, leaders must do the same in our organizations. We must tap into this well of stories and share them, because they eventually evaporate into the atmosphere only to come raining down again and again. After all, they are *our* stories.

HOW TO USE THIS BOOK

This book is about panning for gold. Not gold in the real sense, but the gold we find in our work, our communications, and our relationships. Gold that people share with each other and that illuminates ways to perform better and have more fun.

It is my hope that you use this book both as a set of ideas and as a set of tools. The book is a paperback by design, and as such it is meant to be carried around, written in, and referenced. The stories in this book are meant to ignite your imagination—to get you thinking about *your own stories,* why they matter, and where they will help you take positive action.

The book is organized into four parts. Part One begins with a description of the "problem" leaders face, followed quickly by a solution in Part Two. That solution is then put into action in Part Three by a powerful set of tools—the Win Book, Story Matrix, and Story Coach. In Part Four, I focus in on the techniques of using stories in three particular contexts: leadership, sales, and motivation. I believe that these are the three most critical skills in business. We all need a solid combination of these three skills. Think of it this way: Can you think of a great leader who was not also a great salesperson? Or a great salesperson that wasn't a leader or strong motivator?

The best way to read this book is, predictably, from start to finish. That way, you are certain to see how each part builds on the preceding one, and you will get your arms around "the whole story." Reading one part only is certainly an option, but you run the risk of missing some key stories and concepts that you can apply immediately.

HOW TO USE THIS BOOK

Chapter 1	Chapters 2 + 3	Chapters 4, 5 + 6	Chapters 7, 8 + 9
Problem:	**Solution:**	**Tools:**	**Techniques:**
1. Awash in Bits & Bullets	2. Stories Work	4. The Win Book	7. Leadership Stories
	3. Work Stories	5. The Story Matrix	8. Selling Stories
		6. The Story Coach	9. Motivational Stories

FIGURE 0.1 How to Use This Book

That said, each part explores a concept in its entirety. In addition, the story tools described in Part Three function independently of one another. Although I use them as a complete set, you may find one of the three much more in tune with your personal style, and I encourage you to run with that.

The book has several other features to which I want to draw your attention. There are, of course, lots of stories. I have used stories to elucidate certain concepts and simultaneously provide a demonstration of why stories "work." You will find many of these stories set apart from the main body of the book with a special gray background. You will also find several definitions that I use to frame the problems we face as leaders. Similarly, I have included many pictures that are designed to provide another way to access and think about these ideas. Pictures are just stories too. I'm fortunate to have a mentor who always draws me pictures to help me understand and make sense of what is happening, and so in that spirit I share these pictures with you.

> "And if a picture is worth a thousand words, a metaphor is worth a thousand pictures."
>
> — DAN PINK[2]

The final page of the book is *your* Story Matrix, which is discussed in-depth in Chapter 5. This personal Story Matrix is designed to be completed as you progress through the book.

Finally, as I've immersed myself in the study of what makes great leaders, the many leaders I have met in my travels and the many authors whose books I've read have inspired me. You will find many of their thoughts in the margins of this book. All of these different elements are also indexed in the back of the book for ease of reference. I hope you find these additional features helpful in further exploring these ideas.

This book is not an empirical exercise. The ideas, stories, and tools have grown out of firsthand experience working with leaders and their organizations to capture and tell stories in order to enhance performance.

It is my sincere hope that you have at least several "aha!" moments as you read this, as that is the standard for which I read and recommend books and ideas. And because this work is not empirical, I encourage you to let me know if these ideas fail (or succeed!) in practice.

Finally, I have several other hopes for you. I hope you enjoy this read. Some of my favorite stories are here. I hope they make you laugh and cry and think. I hope this book inspires you to turn your stories into a competitive advantage. And I hope that you use your stories to build better relationships and have more fun.

Be a source of stories. This is the best way to succeed, and the best way to live well.

PART ONE

There is a problem we are all facing, and it's sneaky and subtle and hard to see, even though it's right in front of our faces. The problem is information and its effect on how we communicate and how we live.

You have heard this before. Many pundits, from Neil Postman to Richard Saul Wurman and even Ted Koppel, have decried "information overload"—how technology and media saturation continue to fill every crack and crevice of time, and how it is becoming increasingly difficult to determine what is truly important in our communications. They have pointed our ever-diminishing attention span to how our access to, and facileness with, information has increasingly segmented our time into smaller and smaller pieces. Our lives (and even our children's lives) and our work are overly scheduled and fragmented.

I want to begin this book with a clear definition of the problem that leaders face as we try to lead people and organizations effectively. As leaders, we need to be cognizant of this problem because it is something with which we are all grappling. And because how we manage information has a profound impact on how we communicate, plan for, and reach our goals, we need to be prepared to be part of the solution.

But it's only until we understand the situation we are in, that we can begin to look at it differently. We are surrounded—literally—by a never-ending stream of information. Increasingly, it will be our ability to manage this constant information flow and to make meaning out of these fragments that will allow us to be successful in the near future. And the near future is today.

CHAPTER 1:

AWASH IN BITS
AND BULLETS

Upon this gifted age, in its dark hour,
Rains from the sky a meteoric shower
Of facts...they lie unquestioned,
uncombined.
Wisdom enough to leech us of our ill
Is daily spun, but there exists no loom
To weave it into fabric.

— EDNA ST. VINCENT MILLAY[1]

CLICK, CLICK, CLICK...

In life and in business, we are awash in "bits and bullets." Bits and bullets are data. Facts. Bullet points on slides. Computer screens full of information. Headlines and scores ticking across the bottom of our televisions 24/7. A constant stream of ads and pitches and talking heads. Sometimes it feels like life has become one big infomercial. And the constant stream of bits and bullets doesn't stop when we get to work. In fact, it accelerates. As leaders, most of us have never met an e-mail device or a PowerPoint slide we didn't like. Because technology makes communicating in bits and bullets so easy, we unleash the flood.

No question about it, leaders have a tough job. We are asked to deliver better performance through our people, implement the latest systems, manage goals, communicate and embody company values, and hundreds of other things. We are brokers of information. Leaders above us hand down information we need—division goals, new systems information, competitive data, new products—and then we translate that information, communicate it to our people, and perform against the goals.

Leaders of every stripe, from senior executives and middle managers to salespeople and consultants, spend an inordinate amount of time creating and brokering information, but we spend far less time standing back from that information and asking, "What is the best way for me to communicate this?" *Not asking this critical question too often results in the creation of just more bits and bullets.* That is, we use the same communication methods we always use the same way we always use them, which means that we whip out the laptop, throw together some slides, call a meeting, and then it's click, click, click.

NUMBERS OR LIVES?

A couple of years ago, I was at a meeting where Ray Gilmartin, the CEO of Merck, was speaking. The purpose of his talk was to discuss how the economy and regulation were affecting the drug industry. Leading into some of the main points of his talk, he wanted to make sure that people in the room had a strong sense for what Merck had contributed to the world through the company's development of critical, lifesaving drugs. What happened next was a perfect illustration of the power of stories.

Ray Gilmartin talked about the company's philanthropy and the amounts that had been given to certain causes. He outlined the drugs, such as Mectizan, that Merck had developed to treat river blindness, and the company's antiretroviral program to fight HIV/AIDS in Africa and China. Thus began a long list of impressive accomplishments, and as he talked about them, he gave specific numbers for each; 800,000 vaccines of this in Botswana, 1.4 million vaccines of that in the Americas; and list went on.

These were amazing numbers and any company would be very proud. But what was fascinating was how the crowd reacted. He was losing his audience. As he rattled off more and more numbers, people started to tune out. We were getting lost in the bullet points and losing the true value of the message itself. Instead of being duly impressed with the number of lives saved, we were wondering when he would stop.

Then he did stop. Ray Gilmartin became reflective as he stood on the stage; he paused, and then he related this story: Back in 1942, there was a young woman who contracted an infection after a miscarriage and had been hospitalized in Connecticut for a month. For the entire month, she had been running a fever as high as 105 degrees and was in and out of consciousness. Her doctors were desperate to find a treatment for her, but nothing worked. This young woman was going to die. One of her doctors remembered talking to a colleague about an experimental treatment that was largely unsuccessful, but it was worth a try. The doctors managed to secure a small sample from a lab at Merck—half of what existed in the United States at the time. They tried it. This woman, Anne Miller, became the first person in the United States to receive this new drug, penicillin. And it saved her life.

When Ray Gilmartin finished this story, the audience was completely quiet. We were all picturing in our mind's eye this young woman and the tragic fact that she was going to die. We were picturing our own families and we could feel pain for her family. We were relieved when we were told that she survived and that this new drug had saved her life. This tiny little story had a huge impact. It brought home to us what companies like Merck do. They develop drugs that save people, and all of the statistics in the world about lives saved are not as meaningful as that short story about one person. The story brought each of us into the problem. It created a context to which we could relate. It created an emotional response from us. We could feel it. And it was a great illustration of the difference between stories and bits and bullets.

Our leaders want us to know certain things. They want us to know how to serve customers. They want us to know the mission of the company and how it makes money. They want us to know how to treat each other. In the story above, Ray Gilmartin wanted us to know what Merck cares about and the company's commitment to taking care of people.

In the first part of this Merck story, we are awash in bits and bullets. At some point in presentations like these (usually in the first five minutes), we are lost in the minutiae, drowning in data. That's when we all begin to daydream about lunch or that last vacation we took.

But here, Ray Gilmartin snapped us back from oblivion with a great story. One of the things we will see in the coming pages is that it's the lessons contained in the story that we remember, not the bits and bullets.

"Like desperate Gullivers, we're pinned down by too much information and too much stuff. By one estimate, the world produced five exabytes (or quintillion bytes) of content in 2002—the same amount churned out between 25,000 BC and AD 2000. Little wonder that *Real Simple* has been the most successful magazine launch in a decade, and the blogosphere is abuzz over the season's hottest tech innovation: the Hipster PDA (15 index cards held together by a binder clip)."

— LINDA TISCHLER[2]

> **DEFINITION: Bits and bullets,** *noun:* **1.** Facts and data, parsed into short abbreviations or phrases. **2.** Facts and data devoid of all contexts. **3.** Short bursts of information that can be very useful but also frequently make you say *"huh?"* or *"what the...?"* Usually accompanied by an itty-bitty dot, such as:
> • **This is the bullet of a bit.**

WE ARE ALL FIGHTER PILOTS

The person in Figure 1.1 is you! And me. All of us. This is the way we live now. And it's nothing short of revolutionary how much rich information and entertainment is at our fingertips. If information were food, we would be constantly surrounded by the most outrageous perpetual feast ever created.

Several recent surveys have looked at how people in organizations are dealing with this information flow. One survey found that "the average user spent 3 hours and 14 minutes using technologies to process work-related information—just over 40% of an 8-hour workday."[3] Here's how the average user spent that three-plus hours:

• E-mail—45% of information processing (IP) time
• Telephone calls, conference calls, and voicemail—24% of IP time
• Shared network usage—18% of IP time
• Portal Web site—8% of IP time
• Instant messaging/text messaging—5% of IP time[4]

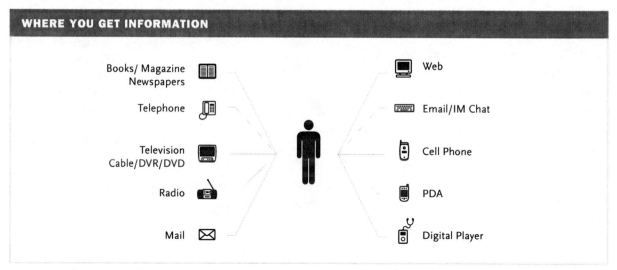

WHERE YOU GET INFORMATION

Books/ Magazine Newspapers — Web
Telephone — Email/IM Chat
Television Cable/DVR/DVD — Cell Phone
Radio — PDA
Mail — Digital Player

FIGURE 1.1 Where You Get Information

The survey results also suggest that less than 50 percent of respondents feel that they are in control of how they manage all of this information. The most surprising finding, though, is that most survey respondents have simply not thought about this issue very much, and thus are not conscious of strategies for managing their personal information.[5] The scary thing is that you are probably looking at these numbers above and thinking, "I *wish* that were me! That 'average user' has it easy!"

Another interesting aspect of this research is that it doesn't look at other forms of technology that we are increasingly using, such as digital music players, digital video recorders, satellite radio, and the Internet. When lumped together with the usual suspects—e-mail, voicemail, and cell phones—it becomes clear that information (and entertainment) is finding and filling every remaining minute of time in our lives.

Surveys like the ones noted above suggest that the pendulum is just starting to swing from unmitigated fascination with technology-enabled access to information to the necessity of having strategies for managing information overload and its negative impact on our productivity.

Another sign that the pendulum may be starting to swing back toward the center is the nascent field of interruption science. This branch of study is gaining a lot of attention because it seeks to understand when it's best and most efficient to interrupt a person at work.

Doesn't this strike you as odd? We have so much technology that interrupts us that we are now studying how to use technology to improve the productivity of interruptions! It seems that we have come to the realization that the constant stream of information, along with its inevitable interruptions, needs to be managed proactively just so we can get something done!

Computers, of course, are both the hero and the villain. As Clive Thompson put it, in an article about interruption science in the *New York Times Magazine*, personal computers began life as "little more than glorified word-processors and calculators,"[8] but then things began to change. Thompson continues:

"'*Multitasking*' *was born; instead of simply working on one program for hours at a time, a computer user could work on several*

"I bought a cell phone in 2005. I finally caved. I just didn't want to be known as 'that guy without the cell phone.'"
— TAYLOR HESS[6]

"The information glut is hardly the apocalypse that some imagined might come about at the millennium. The world's not ending, it's just becoming incomprehensible."
— JOEL ACHENBACH[7]

different ones simultaneously. Corporations seized on this as a way to squeeze more productivity out of each worker, and technology companies like Microsoft obliged them by transforming the computer into a hub for every conceivable task, and laying on the available information with a trowel. The Internet accelerated this trend even further, since it turned the computer from a sealed box into our primary tool for communication *(emphasis added). As a result, office denizens now stare at computer screens of mind-boggling complexity, as they juggle messages, text documents, PowerPoint presentations, spreadsheets and Web browsers all at once. In the modern office we are all fighter pilots."*[9]

Fighter pilots indeed. Organizations make incredibly large investments in technology. What is the purpose of all of these systems and devices? To help us perform better, of course. What other reason could possibly justify the spending?

Given the focus on information technology investment in the average organization, it often seems that we put much more effort into selecting systems and devices than we do in understanding how they will actually help us communicate and perform better.

> "To perform an office job today, it seems, your attention must skip like a stone across water all day long, touching down only periodically."
>
> — Clive Thompson[10]

SO, HOW *DO* WE COM-MU-NI-CATE?

Several important trends are having a profound impact on the way we communicate with each other. First, as stated above, technology has given us many *ways* to communicate. Second, we are now working in many different places (and often alone). Third, globalization and technology have come together to enable us to work remotely and get things done from the car or airplane or basement office, and communicate in myriad different ways. Finally, layers of management have been consolidated and many of us serve as both leaders of others *and* individual contributors.

> "Imagine what we could accomplish if we spent the same time, energy, and money to use the information skills we already know as we do on the tools and technologies otherwise labeled as Information Technology."
>
> — Nathan Shedroff[11]

Of course, these trends can have a positive impact on competitiveness by allowing each segment of work to find the lowest available costs. They are also changing how we communicate, in ways both good and bad.

It's convenient that we can call from the car on the way home to see whether we need any last-minute groceries. It feels more secure to know that our kids and our parents have immediate access to us if they need us. And it's energizing to be able to collaborate with talented people no matter where they are in the world.

There is also a downside—a downside that people are just beginning to realize. These new ways of communicating have changed *the content* of our communications. Almost without realizing it, we have begun to communicate in bits and bullets.

And now we're addicted. Like any addiction, after a while it becomes hard to imagine a future without this new stuff. Over time, our behaviors change and we fall into a predictable, repeated pattern. If you are one of those people who say, *"I'm not addicted. I can stop if I want to,"* just recall the last time you were caught checking your e-mail while someone was talking directly to you. Gotcha!

In an organization, rules for communication are established the same way as rules that govern any community of people. Social conventions, norms, and accepted ways of communicating are built up and when one becomes part of that community, one must live by those rules. This socialization is beneficial in that it helps us get work done and not have to spend time inventing ways to communicate. We don't have to think too much about it.

But therein lies the problem. Because we don't have to spend time thinking through our communications, we don't. We go back to the usual ways of communicating. And when it comes to high-stakes communications—communications affecting leadership, mission, ethical behavior, and teamwork—we most often find ourselves on the losing side of the battle for hearts and minds. *Many times, leaders lose the chance to ignite the performance of their people because they have chosen the expediency of bits and bullets over a more rich and engaging approach.*

LOTS OF TOOLS, NO BLUEPRINTS

Think for a moment about all of the communications tools at our disposal. We have e-mail, a phone, a mobile phone, a pager or BlackBerry, instant messaging, and text messaging. We also have meetings, conferences, and informal conversations. We spend vast amounts of time learning how to use, program, sync, and troubleshoot our communications tools. We also spend considerable time setting up appointments and managing our calendars.

Once all of these unproductive activities are squared away, do we then turn to our well-thought-out blueprint for how to actually use different tools in different situations so that we can increase

"When the bullets are flying, no one is safe."

— JOHN SCHWARTZ[12]

"A researcher at Microsoft, Mary Czerwinski, has studied how the average computer user behaves and has found them to be "as restless as hummingbirds.... On average, they juggled eight different windows at the same time—a few email messages, maybe a Web page or two and a PowerPoint document. More astonishing, they would spend barely 20 seconds looking at one window before flipping to another."

— CLIVE THOMPSON[13]

"Get to the point...I don't have all minute!"

— ERIC CHESTER[14]

"I sometimes think we have become so obsessed with the means of communication that have been developed, that we have lost all contact with the message that is being conveyed."

— TED KOPPEL[15]

performance? Or do we often fall back on the most familiar and expedient—treating all of our tools like hammers and our communications like nails?

As Figure 1.2 shows, our communications devices can actually push us apart, instead of bringing us together. All of this technology-enabled communication we rely on enables us to stay in our cubicle or office (bunker) *and get work done.* But our devices and tools certainly come with a Faustian bargain. Yes, they speed our access to information and increase our flexibility, allowing us to work wherever we are. But they also take away some of what makes it fun and energizing to work with people; that is, the social interaction and learning we get from each other (especially because we now work all the time).

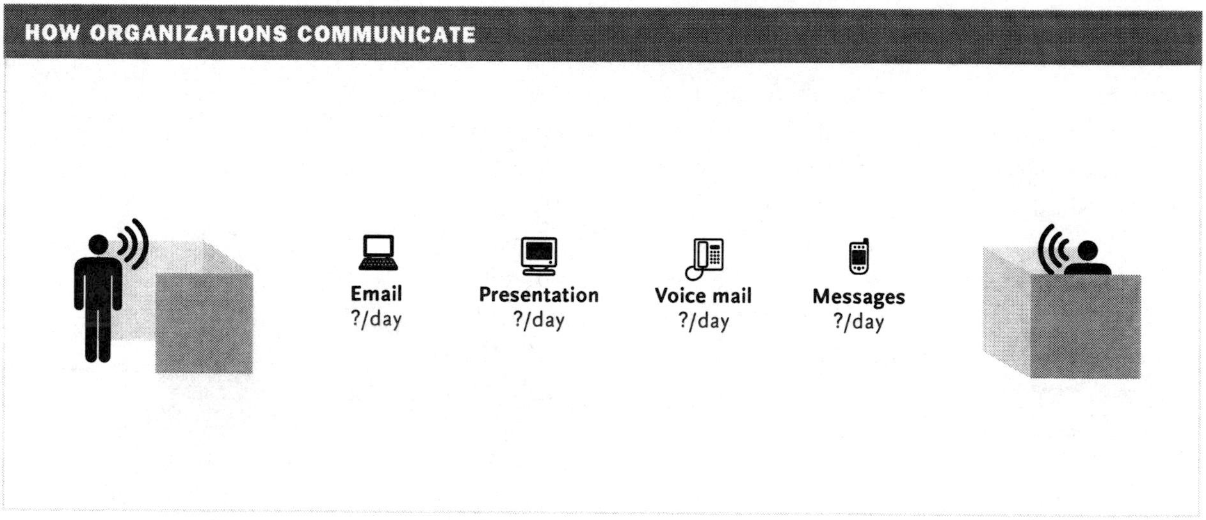

HOW ORGANIZATIONS COMMUNICATE

Email ?/day   **Presentation** ?/day   **Voice mail** ?/day   **Messages** ?/day

FIGURE 1.2 How Organizations Communicate

"It is safe to assume that any individual or group you wish to influence has access to more wisdom than they currently use. It is also safe to assume that they also have considerably more facts than they can process effectively. Giving them more facts adds to the wrong pile. They don't need more facts. They need help finding their wisdom."

— ANNETTE SIMMONS[17]

We have become so incredibly busy sending and receiving e-mail alone that our face-to-face interaction drops like a stone. A client said to me that she asked her employees to turn off their BlackBerrys for a whole day and interact with each other face to face if they needed a piece of information from someone, or needed to convey something. The results were amazing. Her employees told her that they found out so much more about what they needed to know and that it was a lot more fun![16]

One of our main challenges as leaders is to not be like the fish that is oblivious to the water around it. We must take stock of what communication methods we have at our disposal and which one is best suited to the particular task at hand. We should be using a blueprint to determine exactly what kind of communication we will use to impact a specific performance issue.

The **worst** software feature ever invented.

"I need someone well versed in the art of torture—do you know PowerPoint?"

FIGURE 1.3 *New Yorker* Cartoon

FISH TANK FULL OF GLUE

It's 1980 and you just walked into your office and you see the following scene unfold. The boss walks out of his office, past the secretary, down the hall to talk to a colleague. The employee and the boss talk, look at a document together, make a few changes, and then hand the document to the secretary for typing. The employee then calls the customer and tells her secretary that he will have the document to her by next Tuesday.

Don't you get the feeling that all of these people are moving in slow motion? Yuck! It's almost as if they are working in a fish tank full of glue!

Fast-forward to today. The boss in Chicago e-mails her associate in New York, attaching the document that has been edited with tracking. The associate, who is waiting in line at Starbucks, takes out his

"Is there anything so deadening to the soul as a PowerPoint presentation?"

– JOHN SCHWARTZ[18]

The **best** software feature ever invented.

BlackBerry and pages a colleague in Hong Kong (where it's 11 PM) with a quick request for some details. The Hong Kong associate, chatting with some friends in a local pub, feels the buzz of her Treo and responds immediately, after checking some facts on her company's knowledge portal. The associate in New York then accepts the changes to the document and e-mails it to the client. The client, working from home that day, calls the associate's mobile phone to ask him for one final change. The associate pages his boss, she accepts the change, and the client is satisfied.

Isn't this much more exciting? Yes! It's fast-paced, high-tech, and you get the feeling that all of these people are sipping espressos and wearing Armani suits (actually, they are).

What is missing in this story? In the first part of the story, the pace is excruciatingly slow. It is so slow that it's painful to imagine. What's missing are all of the technology enablers that would get the job done faster and the urgency created by a more competitive environment, so the scene plays out in slow motion. What is present, though, is the increased interaction between the people. Because there is a lack of technology enablers, there is more time for interaction, for conversation, and for stories.

This is not to say that today we lack all interaction. We have more interaction with each other than we have ever had before, and a lot of that interaction is a positive development. But, we make far fewer opportunities to share stories, and that's what we need to change. We all seem to be much busier, and technology enables our busy lifestyles. But how do we bring back some of the richness without sacrificing the reach? How do we create relationships that go beyond transactions?

I'm not suggesting that we go back to the olden days. Not at all (I like a good espresso as much as the next guy). But I'm suggesting that we become more aware of our stories, and that we look for opportunities to embed our stories in our communications, because this is great a way to help us manage our information and increase our performance.

"So this is how we end up alone together. We share a coffee shop, but we are all on wireless laptops. The subway is a symphony of earplugged silence while the family trip has become a time when the kids watch DVDs in the back of the minivan. The water cooler, that nexus of chatter about the show last night, might go silent as we create disparate, customized media environments."

– DAVID CARR[19]

SMALL GROWS UP

The march of technology and its effects on our behavior is the same as the story of how "small" became "large." Remember when a "small" was actually small? When you asked for a small coffee, it came in a cute little cup. When you asked for a small Coke, you got a small Coke. But then small grew up, got bigger, started putting on weight, and never looked back. Whether that "small" was a coffee, a soda, restaurant portions, football players, cars, or even suburbs, your first thought was probably, "Wow, this is great. I am getting so much more for my money!" So we order all of those smalls and larges and we feel like we are really getting a deal until we suddenly realize that none of our pants fit! It costs us $60 to fill up our gas tanks and our 25-minute commute is now and hour and a half. Maybe we've had too much. When did that become acceptable? And how long does it take us to realize that some of this stuff is bad for us?

The late Neil Postman once compared our inability to deal with the vast amounts of information pouring over us to the AIDS epidemic. He said the following in a speech in 1990:

"[That is,] we don't know what information is relevant, and what information is irrelevant to our lives. Second, we have directed all of our energies and intelligence to inventing machinery that does nothing but increase the supply of information. As a consequence, our defenses against information glut have broken down; our information immune system is inoperable. We don't know how to filter it out; we don't know how to reduce it; we don't know to use it. We suffer from a kind of cultural AIDS."[20]

"In reality there has not been an information explosion, but rather an explosion of non-information, or data that simply doesn't inform."

– Richard Saul Wurman[21]

Anyone who has used a cell phone, pager, or BlackBerry knows what Postman was talking about. We have all felt the crush of information overload. Anyone who has gone into an hour-long meeting and come out to find 35 new e-mails has felt it. Anyone who has witnessed a 95-page PowerPoint presentation has felt it. And anyone who has had to explain to their spouse why they are bringing the laptop on vacation has felt it.

I put a slightly different (and more positive) characterization on our inability to deal with the deluge of information. I believe we have created for ourselves another incredibly widespread disorder called "story deficit disorder," or SDD. Like attention deficit hyperactivity disorder (ADHD or, more commonly, ADD), SDD causes leaders to jump from one communication or task to the next without thinking through the impact they are having on their own performance or the performance of their people.

> **DEFINITION: Story deficit disorder (SDD),** *noun:* **1.** Common disorder caused by misuse of bits and bullets and resulting lack of stories; symptoms include disorientation, stress, information overload, numbness of the thumbs, immediate onset of narcolepsy at company meetings, rampant sarcasm, and cynicism. Recommended treatment: become a farmer. If farming is not an option, demand more stories in all aspects of your work and life.

Although a bit tongue-in-cheek, there's a very real drawback to story deficit disorder. Because people bounce too frequently from one thing to another and their attention span is shorter and shorter, people pay less attention to the communications that really matter. And when, as leaders, we can't reach our people with an important change, performance of the organization suffers and our own performance suffers.

BUILDING MUSCLE, NOT FAT

Over the past 20 years, we have figured out how to put most of what happens in business in a system of some sort, and the beauty of this is that it makes things like sales performance, claims processed, call times, and delivery schedules much easier to measure. But the challenge we have created for ourselves is that the muscles (our people) that hold the skeleton (our systems) together are really hard to measure. Building those muscles requires what I call "performance skills."

"It's hard to remember that movies were once just a high-tech gimmick under the control of the engineer. Movies didn't flourish until the engineers lost control to the artists—the writers, actors, musicians, and directors (Heckel, 1984). Thanks to their imaginative manipulation of technology, a film's content now transparently connects to our minds."

– Marty Siegel[22]

"It's the people, stupid. You can take any management discipline from the past few years: total quality, reengineering, enterprise-resource planning, and now CRM. In every one of those instances, the failure has been addressing behavioral issues."

– Paul Cole[23]

DEFINITION: Performance skills, *noun:* **1.** Hard-to-quantify skills like leadership, ethical decision making, teamwork, coaching, giving and receiving feedback, building client delight, strategic selling, negotiating, business acumen, sharing insights, and inspiring the true "muscle" of business. Skills that require judgment and a high EQ. Skills that require constant practice and reinforcement through leadership, mentoring, strong communications, powerful learning solutions, and a little bit of luck.

DEFINITION: Showing up skills, *noun:* **1.** Easy-to-quantify skills that come "stock," such as computer skills, basic communications, presentation and project management skills, honesty, and integrity. **2.** The "please" and "thank you" skills that every employee (and every person) should "show up" with.

In Figure 1.4, we see how bits and bullets have a diminishing impact on performance. To expose people to information such as policies and procedures, there is nothing better than bits and bullets. But as we expect people to *build new skills or apply their existing skills* to a new situation or set of goals, we must move into story territory.

Just as we often shape our messages into bits and bullets to accommodate our devices, many companies have organized their communications and learning solutions in such a way as to accommodate technology, not the other way around. For example, just like most companies bought CRM systems, many organizations have now purchased and installed a "learning management system," or LMS. The purpose of an LMS is to, of course, manage learning by distributing and tracking courses taken and compliance achieved.

Systems like these offer some clear benefits, such as providing a common access point to materials, logistical information, and training for hard skills (e.g., using a spreadsheet program or CRM system).

One of the unintended consequences of these systems is that performance skills are now treated like a discrete item (think call times, packages delivered, or number of employees that have completed diversity training). That is, LMS systems only work well when they are acting like databases. ("We know Bill took this course and when, and we even know how he did on the final quiz.")

> "We have spent all of this money and built all of these systems to house information and 'learning' with the expectation that we are creating value. What we've created instead are just corporate landfills."
>
> – Marty Siegel[24]

APPLICATION OF STORIES

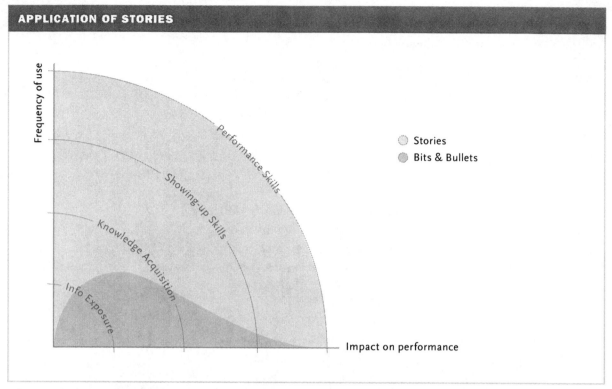

FIGURE 1.4 Application of Stories

WHY ARE WE GOING SOFT?

In the consulting and learning businesses, we are our own worst enemy. In an attempt to appear more credible, we create language that makes no sense to business leaders. We refer to skills as competencies and we build elaborate learning management systems that are just expensive repositories that further undermine our credibility. But the worst offense of all is when we refer to any skill that is not technology-driven—a "hard" skill such as learning to use Microsoft Excel—as a "soft" skill. It's no wonder businesspeople don't take their own learning professionals seriously. The terms we use make it sound like we are building fat instead of muscle! These soft skills aren't soft at all; they are the "performance" skills and muscle that enable organizations to grow and succeed.

But what if the performance skills that are most critical to our success and our organizations don't lend themselves to being easily tracked and measured? Then we have to find a way to build these types of skills and make our technology work for us.

This is one of the keys to being a leader (and high performer) in our time: We are moving so fast and juggling so much that we must make time to distinguish between information that can be trusted to bits and bullets and information that demands a story. You read that right: we must make time. But before you throw this book into the cardboard box marked "Sell on eBay," read on. This book's purpose is to convince you that there are powerful tools at your disposal—indeed, some you may already use—that will *save you time and make you perform better, in business and in life.* A tall order? Certainly. And the journey begins with making the critical distinction between bits and bullets and stories.

"So far, for 50 years, the information revolution has centered on data—their collection, storage, transmission, analysis, and presentation. It has centered on the 'T' in IT. The information revolution asks, What is the MEANING of information, and what is the PURPOSE?"

– PETER DRUCKER[25]

CHAPTER 1:
SUMMARY

THE BITS AND BULLETS

- If we are not careful and cognizant of how we are brokering information, we can overwhelm ourselves and our people and cause performance to suffer.

- Learn your vocabulary words!
  - Bits and bullets—data, facts, and information without context
  - Performance skills—the true muscle of business
  - Showing up skills—the dowry you bring to your job
  - Story deficit disorder—lack of stories to aid learning

- PowerPoint is not evil, but it often brings out the worst in us.

- With the information we have at our fingertips, we are all fighter pilots now. We may look and feel cool surrounded by all of this technology, but what counts is the target.

- We have a choice. We don't have to perpetuate the bits and bullets. There is another way.

THE PICTURES

Where You Get Information
You're surrounded!

How Organizations Communicate
Technology and information can push us apart

The "Delete" button and the "Reply All" button
The good and evil of communications!

***New Yorker* Cartoon**
Too many bullets is painful

Application of Stories
Be aware of your "mix" of stories and bits and bullets

THE STORIES

Numbers or Lives?
Ray Gilmartin's story about penicillin

Fish Tank Full of Glue
We all want to be cool and important

Small Grows Up
Sometimes, what looks like a great deal is exactly the opposite

Why Are We Going Soft?
Talk about performance skills, not soft skills

Chapter 1:
MY THOUGHTS AND IDEAS

PART TWO

The solution to one of the biggest issues we face in today's organizations is innate—it's inside all of us. As human beings, one of our gifts is the ability to share stories and, in fact, this is how we have learned for thousands of years. It is only until recently that the majority of our learning and communications has come in the form of bits and bullets.

When it comes to performing better, there are many reasons that stories are the most effective way to increase performance. Chapter 2 looks at the ten main reasons why stories "work," and provides many examples of the types of connections that stories help leaders make. With the help of many stories, anecdotes, and illustrations, Chapter 2 makes the case that leaders should consider stories to be one of the most powerful tools in their "leadership toolbox."

Leaders make critical distinctions every day. We decide, say, the relative value of different types of investments, or the advantages and disadvantages of focusing our sales efforts on a particular market. Chapter 3 discusses the distinctions we must make when we communicate these decisions. That chapter also tackles some of the bad decisions we make based on our bias for action. Several illustrations make it clear how the different "filters" we take for granted actually impinge on our ability to communicate well. Finally, Chapter 3 looks at the various ways that stories are used inside organizations to cut through the clutter and noise and give people an opportunity to truly perform.

2

CHAPTER 2:

STORIES WORK

PEOPLE ARE BULLETPROOF

How many e-mails do you get every day? How many phone calls? How many instant message chats do you have? Added together, it's probably over 100. When I say this to audiences, most people start laughing and then they start crying! Do you feel like you are getting more done? Sometimes it feels like we are so busy "coordinating" that we've stopped "performing." We are trading a lot more information and we are soaking up less.

The sooner we realize that people are bulletproof—immune to the constant barrage of bits and bullets—the better leaders we will be. Leadership is a lot about influence. Heck, *life* is a lot about influence. We spend an inordinate amount of time persuading and influencing our teachers, kids, clients, bosses, employees, and peers to take an action, whether it be to get an A, do their homework, close a sale, or stretch to reach a goal.

In business, much of persuasion is throwing bullet points at people in an attempt to win their hearts and minds via intellectual argument. Facts and data are presented to give a business case for why something is true and must be acted upon. Because almost all persuasion in business is limited in this way, the facts and data you are presenting compete head-on with the facts and data that are

"Facts are neutral until human beings add their own meaning to those facts.... The meaning they add to facts depends on their current story. People stick with their story even when presented with facts that don't fit. They simply interpret or discount the facts to fit their story. This is why facts are not terribly useful in influencing others. People don't need new facts—they need a new story."

– ANNETTE SIMMONS[1]

already present in people's heads. Your people may be listening as you state your case, but all too often they are thinking: *Yeah, right. I've heard this before. But nothing really ever changes.* So, forget about capturing their hearts. And without hearts, you can probably write off minds as well.

Robert McKee, the Hollywood screenwriting coach, said in a *Harvard Business Review* article: "The other way to persuade people—and ultimately a much more powerful way—is by uniting an idea with an emotion. The best way to do that is by telling a compelling story."[2]

What's fascinating about leadership in business is that most leaders that I've come across *know* that they aren't making a connection. Leaders understand at a fundamental level that the bits and bullets aren't hitting home, because they are just bouncing off of people's existing attitudes, biases, and beliefs.

Leaders often make two false assumptions that cause performance to suffer. First, they assume that their employees are always rational, unemotional, and analytical actors in this numbers-driven game called business. Not on your life. People are messy. We come to work with differing backgrounds, attitudes, and belief systems. We want different things. And none of us use the same "model" to interpret information coming at us, because our interpretation depends on our prior life experiences.

> "Stories are how we remember; we tend to forget lists and bullet points."
> — ROBERT MCKEE[3]

Second, leaders often assume that the information they are communicating is simple and thus should be easy and quick to communicate. Nope. One of the reasons that leaders often fail to communicate even "simple" information is that it's not simple. *They* have had time to think it through, socialize it, and move forward. But no one else has, and thus it's not at all simple for people. Even simple changes need time to be talked about, weighed, socialized, and, finally, adopted or discarded. Imagine a metaphorical dumpster behind your office containing all of the well-intended but discarded attempts to change behavior and enhance performance. How big would it be?

If our success in life and in business depends on how well we influence people, then we had better choose wisely when deciding how to approach them. This is where stories are starting to gain traction and play an incredibly powerful role.

GAINING TRACTION

Stories take many shapes inside organizations, from hallway conversations and e-mail anecdotes to personal stories, corporate legends, and even full-blown, highly produced videos and presentations. And as more and more leaders realize that their communications are not getting through, they are looking to stories as an alternative.

ETHICS, ANYONE?

After months of effort, a group of attorneys from one of the largest auditing firms in the world had just put the final touches on a 65-page document. The document had gone through hundreds of drafts, been reviewed by countless company executives, and made its way through a rigorous approval process. Because the document was critical to the future success of the company, the CEO and his senior management team wanted the document in the hands of all 33,000 employees of the firm immediately.

But the company faced some major problems. First, the document was 65 pages in length—too much for an already overloaded professional to read and understand. Second, this document was no John Grisham novel. It was dry, procedural, and written in the legal language of attorneys. Third, the company's leadership had an audacious goal for this document; its purpose was to affect a major change in how each individual in the company behaved when faced with an ethical dilemma. Because this company had watched competitors crumble under the weight of ethics scandals, its leaders had a high degree of urgency to protect the firm.

To save time and money, the leadership team was tempted to just e-mail the document to all employees, support it as best they could in meetings and company communications, and hope for the best. But they knew better than to do that. They knew that if the employees didn't truly understand the contents of the document, why it was important, and how to behave differently, the firm would be at much greater risk.

So what did they do? They told stories. They told stories of partners asking managers to bury the hours from one client into another client's fees. They told stories of managers asking clients for inappropriate favors. They told stories of analysts and consultants photo-

"In a business setting, a PowerPoint slide typically shows 40 words, which is about 8 seconds' worth of silent reading material. With so little information per slide, many, many slides are needed. Audiences consequently endure a relentless sequentiality, one damn slide after another. When information is stacked in time, it is difficult to understand context and evaluate relationships."

– Edward Tufte[4]

copying and sharing the answer key to continuing education classes. They told stories of clients taking partners to gentlemen's clubs by the airport. They told stories of administrative assistants sharing inside information to stock-trading friends at a backyard barbecue.

These stories were sent to all 33,000 employees. But they didn't stop there. In the middle of each story, they would ask employees: What would you do if you were in this situation? They asked employees to think through how they would address the partner in the elevator or the client who suddenly pulls into the parking lot of a gentlemen's club. They also provided employees with a problem-solving model and asked them to apply it to all of these situations.

And what happened to the 65-page document that outlined all of the policies and procedures? Was it a waste of time and money? Not at all. The key points of the document drove the creation of these fictional, but real-life stories. The stories connected back to the document and showed why certain behaviors are unethical. The document became a key supporting resource instead of the main event.

To date, the company has been very successful in helping employees understand how to take action with the ethical problem-solving model. The company also got an unexpected bonus: it is now winning large clients based on its unique and marketable approach to solving this complex problem. In fact, the company's employees are talking about the stories. They are repeating the stories at work and telling their clients about their unique experience. Because of the success they have had with ethical decision making, the company is now looking at how to apply stories to other challenges, such as improving its client service, increasing sales of large engagements, and building leadership skills.

In short, the company turned a dry, boring e-mail into stories and the stories into results. Stories became the link that turned routine compliance into an experience.

As evidenced from examples like the one above, the use of stories as a leadership tool is gaining recognition and getting traction. Tom Peters is talking about it. *Harvard Business Review* is writing about it. Academia is studying it. And, increasingly, business leaders are learning and using it.

Stories are in the middle of an important migration from being considered too folksy or "soft" for business to being discussed as serious leadership tools in the very serious pages of publications like *The Economist, Fortune,* and *Harvard Business Review.* What these publications and many other business leaders and academics are finding is that our messages and communications, even inside our own organizations, now have to compete with so many more sources of information. So stories, after spending many years being ridiculed as "soft" or "fluff," are gaining respect as tools that just might help these leaders get performance enhancements to stick.

Consider for a moment another business tool that was once widely criticized and often referred to as "a toy" by serious business leaders. This tool was ridiculed by much of the media as being unfit for serious work. It was thought of as a poor alternative to the much larger, more powerful tools used by successful organizations. And it was thought of as a plaything that only kids would use and enjoy. This tool is the PC, and it is now as ubiquitous as the air we breathe. No serious business would last a day without the PC. (As a former IBM salesperson selling midrange systems before the widespread adoption of the PC, I too was guilty of referring to the PC as a toy.)

It is curious that stories are gaining traction now. Many of the world's top business schools like Kellogg, Harvard, and the University of Chicago use stories to teach their students complex topics. But instead of *stories*, these schools use the term *case studies.* However, there is an important difference between case studies and stories.

The difference between case studies and stories is the same as the difference between narrative and stories. A narrative is the explanation of a sequence of events or actions that happened to someone or something. A story, by contrast, adds a layer to narrative by including elements that make people care about the action, such as how someone in the story was affected, the emotions involved, and possibly even the "values" of the people involved in the story.

"Many true statements are too long to fit on a PP (PowerPoint) slide, but this does not mean we should abbreviate the truth to make words fit. It means we should find a better way to make presentations."

– EDWARD TUFTE[5]

A CASE STUDY IN STORYTELLING

While attending business school in 1993, I took a class called "Entre-preneurial Finance," taught by a smart, imposing professor named Steve Rogers. If Professor Rogers was anything, he was intimidating. He knew his subject cold, and he loved to find out if you knew the subject as well as he did by calling on you and sticking with you until he had wrung you dry. One night, Steve had put only one foot into the classroom when he loudly demanded of some poor, lost soul, "ROB-ERT, TELL ME ABOUT THE CASE!!!" As Robert's life undoubtedly flashed before him, he began to mutter some unintelligible grunts and groans about the entrepreneur who, in the case study, had just formed a company and raised a couple million dollars in loans by mortgaging everything he owned. He told of how the man, married and a new father, had given his creditors personal guarantees on his cars and his house in order to finance his business.

As Steve and Robert unfolded the case study, it quickly became a series of events. The guy raised money, hired few employees, started to build a product, and began to sell it. We dug into the numbers and the competitors for this new business and the discussion became very dry—until Steve started to add color to the case. He asked us: "So, if you were this guy, what would you be saying to your wife around the dinner table as your expenses are piling up and it's becoming hard-er to make payroll? How would you feel looking at your little daughter when you know your house is on the line for this business?"

At that moment, we began to look at this case differently. Sudden-ly, we were in the action, and we had an emotional connection to this entrepreneur. The case came alive and we started to see it as a sto-ry that could end badly. That night, Steve taught us some important lessons about how to (and how not to) finance a new business. More than 12 years on, I don't remember the name of the company, the in-dustry, or the other characters. But I remember the lessons of the sto-ry. And that's the only thing that counts.

This difference between case studies and stories is precisely what great teachers, doctors, and business leaders understand so well. You bring case studies "back to life" by adding the details that connect to what we care about, transforming an otherwise dry sequence of events. As the case unfolds in front of you, a story develops when you talk about what the characters were feeling—what scared them and what exhilarated them. That layer of extra information makes all the difference. It is what helps us engage with the content and what helps us remember.

> "I have argued that a key—perhaps the key—to leadership, as well as the garnering of a following, is the effective communication of a story."
> – Howard Gardner[6]

WHY STORIES WORK

I have worked with many leaders who send the memo and then ask: "Why aren't my people getting it? It's so simple!" My answer to these leaders is also simple: Tell them a story. It does take a little more work up front, but not much. And the downstream benefits far outweigh the up-front costs. Before we explore how to do this, let's look at why stories work.

There are ten main reasons why stories work, and these reasons are why business leaders are warming up to stories as a tool to enhance performance.

> "We value narrative because the pattern is in our brain. Our brains are patterned for storytelling, for the consecutive."
> – Doris Lessing[7]

1. Stories create presence

One of the challenges that leaders are beginning to wake up to is *presence*. When most communication is facilitated by technology and comes in the form of bits and bullets, how can we ensure that we actually have people's attention?

As the pendulum begins to swing and we pay more attention to information overload, many leaders are realizing that stories are a powerful tool that can be used to connect with people in a way that we are present to each other. Because stories are a two-way form of communication, and because they can't be captured in bullet point form, they demand our attention. In a real way, they make us sit still for a minute. And when we give a story our attention, we can question, clarify, and confirm what's taking place so that we walk away with a solid understanding of what's being communicated.

Another reason that stories create presence is because they allow for a much-needed break from our information-drenched day. They give us a chance to pause and catch our breath.

Like the 1929 advertising slogan for Coca-Cola, a good story is "the pause that refreshes." If there is something we truly need in our work day, it is to be refreshed. One of the hardest parts about any job—whether you are the CEO or you are a brand-new employee—is dealing with information overload. Sharing a story with people who normally have heads down pounding away at their jobs creates a space for them to pause, listen, reflect, and integrate what they have heard. Even the most simple of stories creates this space.

If stories are migrating along a path toward being considered serious business tools, then one of the stops along the way is Hollywood. Many business leaders and the publications they read have looked to Hollywood, not for entertainment's sake, but for ideas and methods of storytelling. If the American movie machine has proven anything, it's that people all over the world love a good story. Stories entertain, inform, refresh, and connect us—all good reasons to be present to them.

But why do stories create presence through *connecting* us? Because stories often connect with our emotions—something that bits and bullets never do. Therein lies the key lesson from Hollywood. Stories connect to our emotions. (This is where business leaders usually run away.) A natural ingredient of stories is emotion. If the story involves people, it often involves emotions too. I've seen leaders who are uncomfortable discussing anything with emotion try to "turn off" that component of the story, and the story always falls flat. They have hollowed it out and it no longer rings true. When leaders include the actual emotions of the story—whether their own or those of the characters—people get to see and hear something that they don't often get in business. And it makes a connection to what *they* would be feeling and thinking.

Emotions engage our hearts. We can sympathize with a person in the story who is struggling or scared or tired. We feel joy when the person in the story overcomes her obstacles. These basic human emotions that we experience with stories build a connection to our hearts and a presence that is fundamentally different than the normal business communications aimed at our heads.

"When an idea wraps itself around an emotional charge, it becomes all the more powerful, all the more profound, all the more memorable."

– ROBERT MCKEE[8]

"I'M WITH YOU"

A story I often tell to aspiring entrepreneurs is about the early days of growing WisdomTools. The economy had tanked after 9/11 had taken place. The Enron debacle was in full swing. It seemed as if all of our potential clients were hiding under their desks for fear of being laid off. As a result, no one was buying anything and we were in a deep dive. Without clients, we had no money to make payroll. We had to make very, very difficult decisions to let most of our staff go. It hurt so badly that it felt like we had all been punched in the gut.

After we watched our friends and colleagues go, the remaining members of the team came together to talk. We discussed how hard it was and how bleak the future looked. The inevitable question came quickly: "Craig, is this going to happen again? How soon?" Because I didn't know the answer, I told everyone, "I have no idea. I have no answers for you because I can't predict when this might end." And then we started telling stories. We told stories about when the company got started, and what Marty's (our founder) original vision was. We told stories about the clients we served and the fun we had had.

As the meeting wrapped up and over the next couple of weeks, each remaining person on our team, in their own way, came up to me individually and said: "I'm with you. If this thing ends badly, I'll be there. I just want you to know that. I'm not giving up." I had never had more love and respect for a group of people I worked with ever before. And I never looked at the company the same way again.

2. Stories aren't bullet points

When a leader tells a story, context gets created. Context is what is missing from bullet points. In the transition from our thoughts and ideas to writing (or saying) them as bullets points, all of the context gets stripped away. But context—"seeing" the situation unfold as the story is told—is what enables us to truly understand.

Stories honor the complexity of our lives by showing real situations and all of the messiness of those situations and the trade-offs inherent in them. By contrast, when we strip away the context from situations to get down to the bits and bullets, we oversimplify. By oversimplifying, we remove the real learning and leave people feeling empty.

> "Stories are shortcuts we use because we're too overwhelmed by data to discover all the details."
>
> — SETH GODIN[9]

WHAT LISTING PLEASE?

Using bits and bullets versus telling a story inside an organization is like trying to have a conversation with automated directory assistance. In order to squeeze more costs out of our business units, we talk more often to technology than we talk to humans. Consider dialing directory assistance. Instead of just asking a person to look up a number for us, these systems rely on our ability to pronounce the name correctly. Indeed, this is powerful technology that saves a lot of money, but what these systems don't take into account is your "context" when you are placing the call, such as background noise. When you are sitting in Starbucks and you call 411 (or an airline, rental car company, etc.) from your cell phone, the automated voice says, "What listing?" You reply, "Avis Rent A Car," while in the background the barista shouts "DOUBLE SHOT HALF-CAF SOY VANILLA LATTE—RECALL! ADD SPRINKLES!" The automated voice says, "I'm sorry. I didn't get that. Could you say that again?" It's funny; we build these systems to sound human and they end up sounding confused. All you really want is a real person who can say, "Wow, you must be in Starbucks or something. Did you say 'Avis Rent A Car' or 'Ava's Tent Bazaar'?

The context that is created through the telling of a story allows people to see how the pieces fit together and how decisions get made. The context also helps the listener understand what is important to the teller. In a leadership situation, this is incredibly important. Undifferentiated facts make it extremely difficult for listeners to determine what is truly important, because everything appears important. When faced with "the 25 things we must do right now in order to grow the business," people are paralyzed. Where do I start? How do I know when I've accomplished something? What should I watch out for?

A story's context brings these answers along, and gives listeners a sense of what is most important and what is least important. And that, my friends, may seal the argument for any leaders out there still doubting the power of story. It is, in reality, the ultimate bullet—the one that gets results.

"Ultimately, knowledge worker performance comes down to the behaviors of individual knowledge workers. If we improve their individual abilities to create, acquire, process, and use knowledge, we are likely to improve the performance of the processes they work on and the organizations they work for."
— TOM DAVENPORT[10]

• REDUCE COSTS

The bullet point "Reduce Costs" is probably in the Top 10 Bullet Point Hall of Fame (along with "Better Synergies" and "Leverage Assets"). But, like most bullet points, this one is screaming for context to be added to it.

Brian, a colleague of mine, answered that call with this story. Several years ago, we were putting together a film shoot for a client that involved creating a story for new employee orientation. We were on a very, very tight budget and, much to our chagrin, we quickly discovered that we didn't have all the equipment we needed for the shoot. We needed a boom mic—the large pole with the microphone at the end that's held over an actor's head—for capturing the audio of the movie. These items are very expensive.

Brian priced out all the alternatives, but he was not satisfied by the prices he was finding. So he went to eBay. He found a large, telescoping painter's pole for about $30 and then fashioned a homemade connector on the end, where he placed a normal microphone we already had. Everyone at the film shoot was none the wiser—even the professional actors—as the contraption looked and functioned exactly like the real thing at a fraction of the price.

This is a very powerful example of what "Reduce Costs" actually means, which you can apply to your own situation.

3. Stories build strong relationships

Stories make up our earliest memories. Since there were humans, we have used stories to pass along what we have learned to the next generation. David Snowden, an expert on stories at IBM, has written about stories and their impact on hunter-gatherer populations and says, "This provision of space and time for reflection and attuning members of the tribe to common goals is a key component of their success."[11] As much as we would like to think we are highly evolved creatures, we aren't so different from these ancient peoples in our tendency to learn through stories. Can you imagine one caveman saying to another, "Groc, if you and your team go around to the other side of the mammoth, we will spread our risks, leverage our assets, and thus achieve better synergies." Highly evolved, huh?

"Stories are how we explain, how we
teach and how we entertain ourselves…
and how we often do all three at once."
– ROBERT FULFORD[12]

Stories, by their very nature, cannot be transactional. They require a teller and a listener, and whether or not those people have a relationship, thoughts and ideas get exchanged. The listener honors the teller by giving her permission to tell the story and the teller honors the listener by caring enough to tell the story.

Stories weave together facts and feelings and as we hear stories, we literally make meaning out of them. But it's not just the lessons inherent in the story that cause us to learn, it's the relationships we build through the sharing of stories. Think of a new employee. How does she learn? Does she read all of the manuals and then, using the facts she learned, transform into a high performer? It's unlikely.

New employees are told stories. From the first hour on the job, the existing employees tell stories of what it's like to work in that office. Human resources shows the orientation tape, and the new employee naturally picks up cues for what sorts of behaviors are acceptable in this new place and what is required to get the job done.

But just like in our personal relationships, after the "greatest hits" tape is played out, things can get stale. Here is where the challenge to keep the relationship fresh really kicks in. As in a marriage, new employees experience a "honeymoon" period. But once the honeymoon is over, it's bits and bullets 24/7. Couples sometimes struggle to continue to create stories so they are not just going through the motions. This is the very same challenge that each of us face in our organizations. Once we've learned the ropes and heard all of the stories, it is too easy to fall into autopilot.

One of the reasons people get burned out in a job is not because they are working too hard. It's because they are not inventing any new stories. The hard work has long since caused them to grow a new, tough skin that numbs them to the long hours and harried life. But the lack of new and different challenges, the routine, and the uncertainty about where it ends is what causes them to question their commitment.

MATCH.COM, SPEED DATING, STORIES, AND LOVE!

Two fascinating cultural phenomena shed some light on the power of story. Think about Match.com. Essentially what Match.com does is get all of the "bullet points" out of the way, so you can get to someone's story. Because busy professionals don't have the time to wade through a potential mate's stories to learn if they are compatible, they save time by seeing if the bullet points match! Tall, athletic, likes pets, Croatian, whatever. The bullet points can indicate which story may be worth hearing. Only after the bullet points match up does the storytelling begin! But make no mistake about it; the storytelling is where the relationship is built. "Likes pets" doesn't hold a candle to the story he tells you about rescuing that cute little Dachshund from certain death at the pound. Such things are what love is made of!

With speed dating, everything happens much faster. The "bullet points" become only visual cues and the storytelling starts immediately. It has to be concise and impressive—you better bring your best stuff. Only if the first few stories are winners will you get to stay in the game.

Either way, stories are the building blocks of love. Bullet points just leave you sitting alone on a Saturday night.

Imagine going to a movie with a friend. You watch the movie and then you sit afterward and discuss the movie over a glass of wine or a cup of coffee. What is fascinating is that you both just saw the same movie, right? Not necessarily. Each of us lives in a different context and we interpret things differently. During the conversation with your friend, you discover things about the story that you hadn't noticed. *It is in that collaboration that the learning takes place and a relationship is built.* If someone had handed you a document as you left the movie theater that listed the three things you should take away from this movie, you would probably be offended. Best case, you would say, "Well, maybe. But I see it differently."

As soon as we tell people only what they need to know, we have lost the connection with them. Stories rebuild the connection by engaging people to figure out what's embedded in the story and to let them see it from their perspective. Then, in the interpretation of the story, we find both common bonds and respectful points of difference.

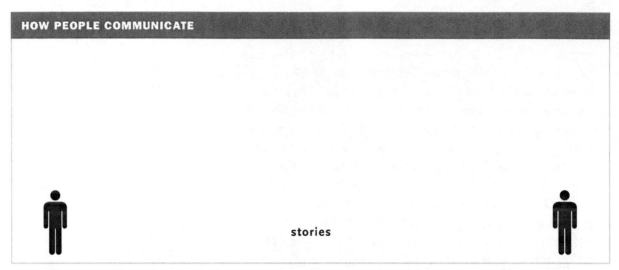

FIGURE 2.1 How People Communicate

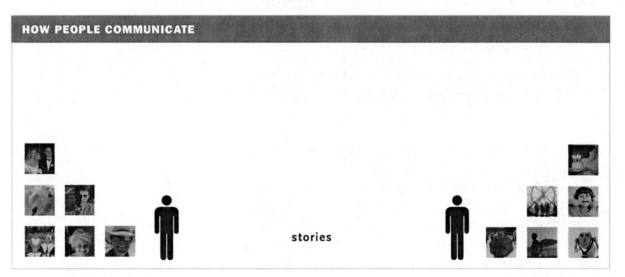

FIGURE 2.1 How People Communicate

HOW PEOPLE COMMUNICATE

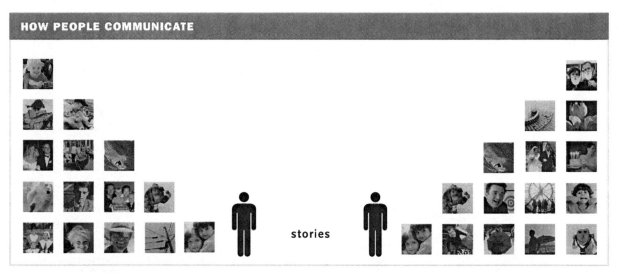

stories

FIGURE 2.1 How People Communicate

I remember discussing a book, *Guns, Germs, and Steel*, with a good friend of mine. He had a completely different perspective on the book and as we debated its merits and shortcomings, his stories and worldview helped me understand both what I appreciated about it and where I thought it could have been better. Without that discussion, I would have had a much more limited view of the content, and I wouldn't have had the chance to build on our relationship.

As leaders, it is our responsibility to help create and tell the stories that keep people growing, stretching, having fun, and performing. One of the many benefits of sharing these stories is illustrated in Figure 2.1 above. Unlike Figure 1.2 in Chapter 1, that illustrated how the devices and ways we communicate can push us apart and put up artificial barriers, stories actually bring us together. When two people meet, they begin to tell their stories. Over time, these stories begin to "pile up behind them," pushing them closer together. In the last part of Figure 2.1, these two people are much closer together than they were before, and, if you look closely, some of their stories are the same—they have shared experiences that have now created a bond between them. The longer we know someone, the more stories we create together.

"Tell me and I forget,
Teach me and I remember,
Involve me and I learn."

— BENJAMIN FRANKLIN[13]

4. Stories illustrate success and failure

Many organizations find it difficult to talk openly about failure. It's often a taboo subject, one best left unsaid. This is a gigantic missed opportunity. Even if this were the *only* valuable element of telling stories, they would still be worth their weight in gold. Business communications almost can't help but describe what success looks like, because we naturally want to reinforce positive stories about others and ourselves.

But stories also demonstrate how failure can happen, and what that will look (and feel) like. When it comes to talking about failure, what stories do particularly well is "protect the innocent." Here's a simple example. In our work with clients, we often craft "failure" stories where all of the characters are fictional, but the failure the story depicts is very real. This way, no one feels picked on. We aren't saying, "Boy, Joe, did you screw that up! Can't believe you still have a job!" Instead, we are saying, "Imagine that Joe is facing this situation. Now, let's say he makes this decision and it blows up in his face! Could that happen?" In a very concrete way, stories outline how failure can happen and how to plan for it.

Many times when people are working through a failure story, they will see themselves in the action. They will remember how they have made that same mistake, how it felt, and what the consequences were. People are drawn to failure stories in the same way we are drawn to accidents. We have a desire to see what happened and to see how to make sure it doesn't happen to us.

Annette Simmons, in her powerful and insightful book, *The Story Factor*, talks about how leaders need to share failure stories and stories of what scares them. Simmons contends that this gives leaders a much stronger connection to their people and that people get a much richer sense of *how* their leaders are thinking through challenges and what they can do to drive the desired results.

Failure stories have even greater benefits beyond the valuable lessons they contain. They convey the power of being honest, courageous, and authentic—and that power is multiplied in the story's transference from the teller to the listener.

5. Stories allow for reflection

Our work lives do not leave much room for reflection. The act of reflection—sitting still and thinking back through choices made and paths followed—gets crowded out by action. It used to be that when we got in the car or on the train, that was our time to decompress and reflect. Not anymore. We are constantly connected

> "A story lets them decide for themselves —one of the great secrets of true influence. Other methods of influence— persuasion, bribery, or charismatic appeals—are push strategies. Story is a pull strategy."
>
> – Annette Simmons[14]

everywhere—even on airplanes. With our handy laptops, Black-Berrys, cell phones, iPods, and satellite radios, we are now "tuned in" 24/7, and this greatly narrows our time to reflect.

Why is this important? Because it is in the process of reflection that we learn. One of the five adult learning principles is "learning is a continuous cycle of action and reflection."[15] But our business culture can be characterized by "Fire. Fire. Fire." rather than "Ready. Aim. Fire." Action? We're the best in the world. Reflection? Not so much.

FIGURE 2.2 A Zigzag Bridge

Japanese gardens are designed to help us reflect and enjoy the experience of being "present." They are full of symbolism. In a Japanese garden, there is often a bridge called a "zigzag" bridge that crosses over to an island in the garden. Many times, the zigzag bridge is made up of two large stones or pieces of granite placed next to each other with only two of the corners touching. As you walk across a zigzag bridge, you have to shift from one piece to the other. There are no railings on the bridge and as soon as you walk across one, you automatically start paying attention to what you are doing because you don't want to fall into the water. *The purpose of the zigzag bridge is to slow you down so you notice more of the garden.*

Stories are like a zigzag bridge. Almost unconsciously, stories make us slow down and listen. Because we are not sure where the story is leading, we listen. As we discover where the story is leading, we begin to bring our own experience to bear on the story—we interpret the story in ways that connect it to our prior experiences. This is how we, as adults, make sense of all the facts, data, bits, bullets, and stories.

This process of learning is much different for kids. Because they do not draw on a vast amount of prior experiences, kids easily absorb much more information no matter what form it comes in. I often say that we just open the tops of kids' heads, pour in tons of information, and it all filters through and sticks (except the part about cleaning up their rooms).

But with adults, it's different. As information gets poured into our heads, it bounces off all of the prior experiences and if it doesn't fit and reinforce what we already know, it bounces out and doesn't stick. This is why Simmons says, "People don't need new facts—they need a new story."[16]

When a story gets "poured" into the head of an unsuspecting adult, the first unconscious question that gets asked is, Have I heard this one before? If the story has been heard before, we listen to see if it will have a different ending, or if the teller has a surprise in store for us.

If it's a new story, we follow along asking ourselves (again, mostly unconsciously): Does this make sense? Do I believe this? What's different about the stickiness of stories is that we get to see, hear, and reflect on the journey that resulted in the conclusions. Instead of the finalized, polished bits and bullets, we see the characters in the story taking action and making decisions in a familiar context, and it becomes easier to relate to why certain things happened. This doesn't mean we agree; it just means that we can relate because we can see how the story unfolded.

It is also in this process of reflection that people, as Wisdom-Tools' founder Marty Siegel says, "bring more to a story than is actually there." I am constantly surprised by how people find lessons and interesting aspects in a story that had not even occurred to me. This is because as people reflect on a story, they bring their own experiences to it, which helps them understand it.

In the world of fast-moving business where we are awash in information, this difference between stories and bits and bullets is profound. In a time when we are building straighter, wider bridges that move us ever faster, stories bring back some of the richness of the journey for which we are longing.

> "Context, from the Latin *contexere*, means to weave together, to engage in an active process of connecting things in a pattern."
>
> – Sam Wineburg[17]

6. Stories are an antidote

If you need an antidote, it means you have already caught a sickness. And we have. Collectively, we have ADD and SDD, and the antidote can't come soon enough. But it won't be given to us. We will have to mix it ourselves. Therein lies one of the many gifts of stories. Because stories both connect us and allow for reflection, they serve as an antidote to the barrage of bits and bullets. We can sit back and listen, decide what the real meaning is in the story, and then take action.

In the popular movie *The Matrix* by the Wachowski brothers, the hero (Neo) gets shot at by the villain (Agent Smith) many, many times. The filmmakers pioneered a cinematography technique they dubbed "bullet time" where they slowed the action down considerably in order to give the viewer a detailed picture of each individual bullet flying through the air. This technique gives the viewer a heightened anticipation of the action, because many scenes have so much action that, without bullet time, the viewer would be left wondering what actually happened.

Stories also slow the action down in order to let us see decisions *as they get made* instead of just being privy to the *results* of the decisions. Stories bring us into the decision process and thereby operate as an antidote to more directives coming down from on high.

7. Stories show the how and why as well as the what

When we create stories for our clients, we bring together our story experts and their subject matter experts and put them through a story-creation process we call "WisdomPath." This process is unlike anything the clients have been through before. They literally create the story about their work and challenges out of what appears to be "thin air." It is a fascinating process to watch, and its result is a fictional story about a very real challenge.

> "Stories are the best way to help people connect the dots."
>
> –Scott Carbonara[18]

But then a funny thing happens on the way to igniting performance. The story gets shared with others, and they begin to interact with it. They express their attitudes toward the characters (who have been designed to look like them) and the decisions that they make. They express consternation about why a character would have behaved a certain way, and they speculate as to why he would do that. This is where the story goes beyond the limited view of its creators. People add their own opinions and ideas, and the story becomes richer, more realistic, and more meaningful. Soon, people are learning more than the story designers ever intended!

The best example of this phenomenon is the Bible. Over the centuries, people have read, re-read, interpreted, discussed, and debated the stories in the Bible. They have added their own meaning to those stories in trying to figure out how these stories relate to their immediate lives.

One of the interesting challenges that we come across in our work at WisdomTools is when we are building a story on a tough subject (say, ethics or leadership). Our clients often ask, "This story is great, but where are the answers?" We respond, "They are embedded in the story!" This response never fails to disappoint a client because they are used to organizational communications *telling you what you need to know.* This is exactly why most communications fail to connect and most learning efforts fall far short.

> "A story will help them figure out what all these facts mean."
>
> – Annette Simmons[19]

Another person who has studied and written about using stories in the context of organizational learning is Roger Schank. He says, "We need to tell someone else a story that describes our experience because the process of creating the story also creates the memory structure that will contain the gist of the story for the rest of our lives. Talking is remembering....But telling a story isn't rehearsal, it is creation. The act of creating is a memorable experience in itself."[20]

8. Stories show multiple perspectives

Because many stories have more than one character, they offer the listener multiple perspectives on a particular challenge. In the same way that stories allow us to see both success and failure, they let us take on the perspective of each character. Why did he do that? What would I do if I were him? How is this going to end?

FIGURE 2.3 *Guardian* Advertisement

A client of ours, the advertising firm DDB Worldwide, produced a fantastic commercial back in 1987. The ad was for the British newspaper, *The Guardian*, and it was shot in black and white in a series of three short clips. The first clip, in Figure 2.3, shows a young man with a shaved head running as fast as he can down a sidewalk as a police car pulls into the frame.

The second clip, in Figure 2.4, shows a different perspective. It shows the same young man from the back as he continues to run down the sidewalk while a businessman in a suit turns to see him coming. The businessman thrusts his briefcase out in front of his chest just as the young man grabs it with both hands.

FIGURE 2.4 *Guardian* Advertisement

The final clip, in Figure 2.5, was shot from the top of an adjacent building and it shows the whole perspective of the scene. In the final clip, the young man is grabbing the businessman's briefcase and using it to shove the businessman out of the way of a falling pallet of bricks above him that would have surely killed him.

This young man, who in the first clip appeared to be a delinquent running from the police and in the second clip appeared to be robbing and assaulting the businessman, turns out to be a hero. He saw the bricks falling and risked his own life to save the man.

FIGURE 2.5 *Guardian* Advertisement

This is a story that plays out on film. But it is a perfect illustration of why stories are such a powerful way to help us understand other people's perspectives. From each character's eyes, or from each situation's challenge, we can ask questions such as: What is happening here? Why is he doing that? What would I have done differently? Because stories illustrate different perspectives, they give people a chance to "get out of their box" and try on someone else's viewpoint. The process of thinking through and questioning these different viewpoints creates understanding, alignment, and commitment.

9. Stories help us unlearn

That's right, *unlearn*. It sounds crazy, but being able to unlearn bad patterns or useless knowledge is becoming more and more important. Just as we have hailed the increased connectivity and the plethora of information at our fingertips, we need to understand the impact of this information overload. Through a story, people get to see what patterns and behaviors don't fit anymore. Here's a simple, autobiographical example:

One day, two salespeople were having lunch with a new client. One of the salespeople was an older veteran of the company and one was a young rookie who was trying to learn the ropes. They operated as a team. The client represented a large potential sale that would make a huge impact on their earnings for the year. The three of them meet at an Italian restaurant near the office at noon. The client and the younger salesperson ordered iced tea and the veteran ordered a martini. As the lunch (and the martinis) wore on, the client became a little uncomfortable and the younger salesperson was not sure how to handle it. The veteran salesperson didn't even notice the discomfort because this is the way he had always "done lunch."

This simple story illustrates a difficult situation and what behaviors may or may not be appropriate by demonstrating the impact that different behaviors have on those involved. For the less experienced employees, it illustrates how things such as client lunches should be handled. For the more experienced employees, it shows the types of behaviors they must *unlearn*. Even this simple, short story with no apparent ending is more effective than its most common replacement, the PowerPoint slide in Figure 2.6.

"Information is now a commodity that is bought and sold; it comes indiscriminately, whether asked for or not, directed at no one in particular, in enormous volumes, at high speeds, disconnected from meaning and import. It comes unquestioned and uncombined, and we do not have, as Millay said, a loom to weave it all into fabric. No transcendent narratives to provide us with moral guidance, social purpose, intellectual economy. No stories to tell us what we need to know, and especially what we do not need to know."

– Neil Postman[21]

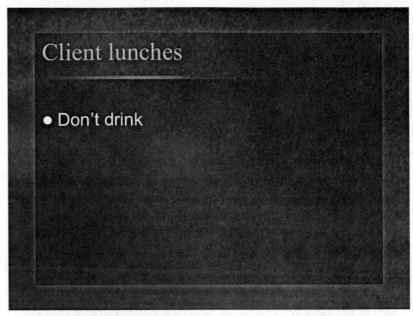

FIGURE 2.6 PowerPoint: Client Lunches

"You know you've been successful as a leader when people start to repeat the stories and the context, and they don't connect it to you."

– RAY ANGELI[22]

"Story is a more dynamic tool of influence. Story gives people enough space to think for themselves. A story develops and grows in the mind of your listener. If it is a good story, you don't have to keep it alive by yourself. It is automatically retold or replayed in the minds of your listeners."

– ANNETTE SIMMONS[23]

10. Stories spread

Have you ever heard someone say, "You are never going to believe the PowerPoint presentation I just saw! Wow!" Probably not, but I bet you have heard someone say, "You are never going to believe the story I just heard." This is because stories spread.

You may be thinking rumors and gossip, and that's the *last* thing you want. It is true that rumor, gossip, and innuendo use the very same powerful elements outlined above, but that is all the more reason to be telling the *right* stories. The right stories that are truthful and contain both success and failure serve to counteract the inevitable negative rumor and gossip that runs through every organization. And in fact, bullet points actually *create* gossip and empty speculation as a natural and desperate attempt to create meaning from the bits and bullets!

Stories spread because they are often told in groups, from 2 to 2,000 and up, and thus they benefit from the social aspect of groups. Malcolm Gladwell, in his groundbreaking book, *The Tipping Point*, explored this concept as he was explaining the nature of epidemics. He writes:

"Anyone who has ever been to the movies knows that the size of the crowd in the theater has a big effect on how good the movie seems: comedies are never funnier and thrillers never more thrilling than in a packed movie house. Psychologists tell us much the same thing: that when people are asked to consider evidence or make decisions in a group, they come to very different conclusions than when they are asked the same questions by themselves. Once we're part of a group, we're all susceptible to peer pressure and social norms and any number of other kinds of influence that can play a critical role in sweeping us up in the beginnings of an epidemic."[24]

Gladwell goes on to talk about how the context that gets created in groups influences individual decisions. So it's not as if we are just caught up in the moment and swept off our feet. We are truly influenced by stories and the fact that they are often told in groups, and this can have a profound impact on the individual decisions we make thereafter as we tell and retell these stories to ourselves and others.

When you were reading the section above, did you notice anything? Did you notice that as I introduced each element of what makes stories powerful, each element was also illustrated in an anecdote, story, or quote? Why is this? Because the alternative would look like the PowerPoint slide in Figure 2.7.

Of course, stories are not the answer to every challenge. There are certainly many challenges that can be tackled quickly and efficiently by bits and bullets. In order to decide when to use the different tools in our toolbox, we must make the critical distinction between high-stakes and low-stakes communications.

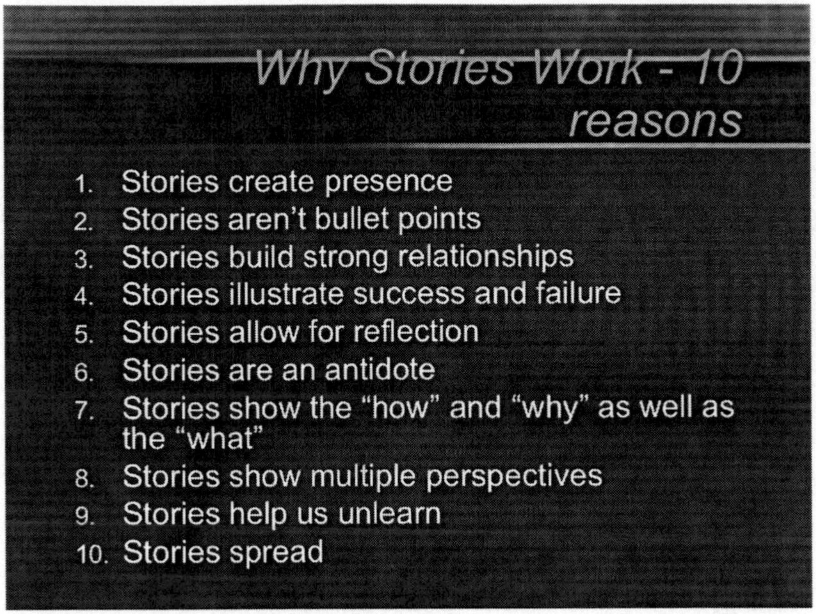

Why Stories Work - 10 reasons

1. Stories create presence
2. Stories aren't bullet points
3. Stories build strong relationships
4. Stories illustrate success and failure
5. Stories allow for reflection
6. Stories are an antidote
7. Stories show the "how" and "why" as well as the "what"
8. Stories show multiple perspectives
9. Stories help us unlearn
10. Stories spread

FIGURE 2.7 PowerPoint: Why Stories Work

Chapter 2:
SUMMARY

THE BITS AND BULLETS

- Leaders make assumptions that are often false:
  - Employees are always rational, unemotional actors in business and, thus, we can just give them the facts and they will perform.
  - The information being provided is simple, so employees shouldn't have any problems interpreting and taking action on it.

- There are ten main reasons why stories work:
  1. Stories create presence.
  2. Stories aren't bullet points.
  3. Stories build strong relationships.
  4. Stories illustrate success and failure.
  5. Stories allow for reflection.
  6. Stories are an antidote.
  7. Stories show the *how* and *why* as well as the *what*.
  8. Stories show multiple perspectives.
  9. Stories help us unlearn.
  10. Stories spread.

THE PICTURES

How People Communicate
Unlike bits and bullets, stories pull us closer together

A Zigzag Bridge
Stories slow down the action so we can actually see what's happening

Guardian Advertisement
The power of context is unequaled when it comes to true understanding

PowerPoint—Client Lunches
We need to stop pretending that PowerPoint slides can help people really learn important, complex issues

PowerPoint—Why Stories Work
A poor alternative

THE STORIES

Ethics, Anyone?
Getting results by breaking the addiction of bits and bullets

A Case Study in Storytelling
Remembering the lessons of a story by adding context and color

I'm with You
Feeling the impact of a story

What Listing Please?
Remember, we are all human

Reduce Costs
What do these bullet points actually mean?

Match.com, Speed Dating, Stories, and Love!
Stories are the building blocks of love

CHAPTER 2:
MY THOUGHTS AND IDEAS

3

CHAPTER 3:

WORK STORIES

"Story has become more important, in part, because of Google. A world of Google means that facts are ubiquitous and free. And so Economics 101 will tell you anything that is free doesn't have much economic value. And therefore what's more valuable in this world of ubiquitous facts is not so much collecting the facts and lining them up in a logical argument because that's relatively easy to do. What becomes more important is the ability to take those facts, put them in context, and deliver them with emotional impact. And that's what story does."

– DANIEL PINK[1]

HIGH-STAKES VERSUS LOW-STAKES COMMUNICATIONS

When we treat all of our communications in the same way, they will be received the same way. Why would we expect our new ethics policy to be treated differently and be taken more seriously if it is communicated the same way as the new travel and expense guidelines? Why would we expect enthusiasm and loyalty from our new employees if we spend the first six weeks they are on the job cramming facts and data into their heads? How do we expect our customer service people to truly engage customers if they are measured by how quickly they get to the next call?

Have you ever seen two people sitting at the same table in a restaurant talking to different people on their mobile phones? Have you ever been in a meeting with someone who gets a page and answers it, only to look back at you and ask, "Sorry, what were you saying?" (By the way, this should be a felony.) Have you ever left the dinner table to check your e-mail? Have you ever brought your e-mail to the dinner table? I admit I have done all of these things. I'm not saying that we should never do these things, but we should be much more aware of how we are communicating *when the content of our communications matters.*

"Business leaders are getting rid of PowerPoint presentations in favor of storytelling, Smith says. 'How can you evoke
an emotion with a bullet point?'"

– Del Jones[2]

Any communications tool, when used correctly, is perfect and powerful. When you need a price for a proposal, send a "page" to your colleague. When you need a phone number, instant message your associate who has it. That is, when the stakes of your communications are low, grab any device that happens to be lying around and fire away! But when you need to lead people, ask people to spend a significant amount of money, change something they have been doing, or motivate and inspire people, put the bits and bullets down and slowly back away. Bits and bullets have no relevance for these challenges, yet leaders make this mistake over and over again.

Why do we do this? Because we are biased for action. Many times, of course, this is a good thing because it means that we are getting the job done. But this bias for action also creates a blind spot between what is truly important and deserves focus and what is not.

A common challenge all leaders face is quickly sifting through what is and what is not important. When we need to influence performance, we should first ask if the situation is a "high-stakes" situation. Is this situation important enough to demand a unique solution?

In order to determine that, we need to discern which types of communications are high stakes and which are low stakes. As shown in Figure 3.1, bits and bullets are better suited to communicating and reinforcing low-stakes communications, such as product information and policies and guidelines. Stories, on the other hand, are critical when it comes to building performance skills,

FIGURE 3.1 High-Stakes versus Low-Stakes Communications

such as leadership, coaching, and client delight. This picture serves as a "blueprint" for thinking through our communications needs and the tools that are available to us.

The skills on the left side of the picture in Figure 3.1 are what I call showing up. These are skills that every employee should bring to the workplace no matter what. Showing-up skills are the fundamentals of communication and baseline skills that we, as employees, are supposed to bring to our workplace the first day we show up. They also represent the infrastructure—the "rules"—that govern our behavior and many of our actions at work. These skills are relatively easy to define and straightforward to communicate. They are the "please" and "thank you" skills of an interaction.

On the right side of the picture are the performance skills that are harder to define, build, and measure because they represent the *how* and *why* of daily work. Leaders often struggle to explain to people the how and why of an issue. Sometimes this is a result of the leader already having "socialized" the reasons for the request and, in the scramble for immediate results, forgetting the how and why.

And sometimes this is due to a perceived lack of time and/or options for getting the message out the right way—a way that people will be able understand and act on the message. This is exactly when the risk of falling back to bits and bullets is the highest.

So what makes a leader's communication high stakes? If you are asking for an action or behavior that involves a significant change or shift in how something currently gets done, consider it high stakes. If you are trying to enhance a performance skill, support a project that the company has spent significant money on, or ask for something that impacts clients or customers, you are definitely in high-stakes territory.

What characterizes low-stakes communication? If the content of your message is mostly informational, or if it is something that represents an infrastructure issue, such as common policies, procedures, and compliance, you are in low-stakes territory.

> "Our tendency to try to create teaching that is clear creates an unintended consequence of oversimplification. When someone understands what you want them to do but doesn't buy into why you want them to do it, you will never be satisfied with their performance."
>
> – ANNETTE SIMMONS[3]

YOU KNOW YOU ARE ABUSING BITS AND BULLETS WHEN...

- You send an e-mail to the person sitting in the office next to you.
- You spend 90 minutes carefully choosing the clip art to accompany your bullet-pointed slides.
- You frequently use your BlackBerry to arrange your next meeting while sitting in your current meeting.
- Your client's e-mail system chokes on a 90-page PowerPoint presentation you are trying to send him.
- You are in a one-on-one meeting, and you lose track of what your colleague is saying because you are reading e-mail.
- You've never actually met 80 percent of the people with whom you work.
- You haven't stopped to consider your choices for communicating some information that will impact your goals or strategy.
- You just spent $500,000 on a leadership team meeting of the top 350 leaders and you had seven speakers, each with a 50-page PowerPoint presentation.
- You make important life decisions based entirely on an e-mail conversation while asking for a triple-shot, skim vanilla latte.
- You page your spouse and he is sitting right next to you.
- You are more upset by misplacing your BlackBerry than not seeing your kids for a week.
- Your thumbs have grown two inches in length in the past year due to typing on your BlackBerry.
- You can't put down your cell phone long enough to rob a bank, so you just keep talking on it while you execute the theft (yes, this actually happened).

It is remarkably easy to get these communications confused. Many times, I've been told by clients, "This compliance issue is huge! If we screw this up, we could be out of business!" But then they create some fancy PowerPoint slides or boring linear e-learning to "teach" employees what they need to know and people end up just clicking through as fast as they can to get to the test. (If you listen closely as you walk the halls during the rollout of one of these initiatives, you will hear the frantic clicking of people trying to just get through this stuff as fast as they can!) This is ludicrous. We are actively fooling ourselves into believing that we are taking these things seriously because we can show a database of test scores and completion. The truth is, most of these compliance-related communications allow employees to take the test as many times as they need to or otherwise "game" the system until they can beat it.

With communications challenges like these, the question we should be asking is, Do I need these people to actually learn this *such that they are going to behave differently*, or can they get by with some passing knowledge of the issues? If the answer is the former, you have a high-stakes communications challenge. Otherwise, go ahead and get out the clip art and polish off those bullet points.

It is our job as leaders to help filter the information that bombards our people. By *filter*, I don't mean *alter*. I mean filter almost in the sense of protecting people from a jumble of meaningless, or unprioritized, information.

"Stories...are what animates our 'reasoning process.'
Stories...give us permission to act.
Stories...are photographs of who we aspire to be.
Stories...cause emotional response.
Stories...connect."

– TOM PETERS[4]

EVERYTHING'S "AWESOME"!

A few years ago, I got some important and timely feedback from my team at WisdomTools during our yearly 360 feedback process. I was your typical overeager and overenthusiastic entrepreneur and I was so excited by the people I was working with and the work we were doing that I often referred to what was happening around me as "awesome." At company meetings, I would often announce a new client or a new accomplishment by the software developers that was truly awesome.

Much to my chagrin, I got strong, unequivocal feedback from nearly every person who contributed to my 360 feedback that I greatly overused the word *awesome*. I was upset and defensive, thinking that I was being punished unfairly and misunderstood, until I asked for an explanation. The first person I asked looked me straight in the eye and said, "Craig, if everything is awesome, nothing is awesome." She stopped me cold, and in that moment I began to think about my communications much differently. I began to be more discerning of what different types of communications each challenge truly required.

Admittedly, this can be difficult to do. As leaders, we are bombarded by information and data ourselves, and most of it looks important. We, in turn, push it out to our people as fast as it comes in. It's almost the same phenomenon we see as parents when we overschedule or overinvolve our kids. It's hard to limit the activities they are involved in, but we know, almost unconsciously, that if they just run breathlessly from one thing to another that they aren't really learning anything in any depth, and they aren't building strong relationships.

We need to make a conscious choice about what is high stakes and what is not. It is only then that we can make better choices about how to use the different communications tools at our disposal and when to use these tools to tell stories instead of send more bits and bullets.

WORK STORIES

Of course, we tell all kinds of stories in organizations. Stories that illustrate what we do, where we come from, and what we care about. We tell stories about the famous deal that was closed just as the company was about to miss payroll, about the founder changing the name of the company after a conversation with a customer, or about how one small incident changed the direction of the entire business.

Stories are being created and are unfolding around us all day every day. Salespeople are coming back to the office and telling us about the client's reaction to the latest product line. Service people are talking about the crazy workaround they discovered when a customer called in with a problem. Senior managers are talking about what will happen if a competitor decides to enter one of their lines of business. And a million other stories, big and small.

In his groundbreaking book, *The Tipping Point*, Malcolm Gladwell profiles the Gore company, and how the company has chosen a very successful, and unique, growth strategy.[5] Gore makes many different types of products from clothing with GORE-TEX® fabric to cables and components to gear for various branches of the military. Its success has brought growth in revenues and people. But Gladwell describes that, unlike most companies that accommodate their employee population with ever-larger facilities, Gore builds offices and facilities that accommodate only about 150 people at a time under one roof.

Because of this self-imposed limit, the company's growth has meant that it has had to build many different offices, often in close proximity to each other. The reason that Gore has chosen to do this can be explained by the Rule of 150. The basis of the Rule of 150 was formed in research by the British anthropologist Robin Dunbar, who found that humans' (and other primates') "social channel capacity"—that is, our brain's ability to process relationships between ourselves and others—has a natural limit of approximately 150 people.[6]

As Gladwell describes it, The Rule of 150 is "a simple rule of thumb that distinguishes a group with real social authority from a group with little power at all."[7] He explains that as a group of people grows larger than 150—be it a business division, a religious organization, or a military unit—the social connections and norms that influence behavior begin to break down. Conversely, in a group under 150, we care enough about what people think of us that it influences how we behave. In the smaller group, Gladwell says that there exists "a kind of peer pressure: it's knowing people well enough that what they think of you matters."[8]

And these social connections are the most powerful influencers of behavior. But what actually makes up these "connections"? What creates the context within which people behave a certain way? One of the most powerful tools is story. The most common communications vehicle in a small group of people is stories. And as we have seen in Chapter 2, stories carry the context, norms, and successes and failures that end up creating the "rules" for our behavior.

Gladwell goes on to describe Gore: "It is a big established company attempting to behave like a small entrepreneurial start-up. By all accounts, that attempt has been wildly successful. Whenever business experts make lists of the best American companies to work for, or whenever consultants give speeches on the best-managed American companies, Gore is on the list."[10]

Organizations like Gore literally build a story-rich atmosphere where stories are shared and repeated, and thus they create the right kind of peer pressure and desire to contribute that helps them be successful. This is exactly the kind of atmosphere that we, as leaders, need to build around us.

"Never underestimate the power of a good story."

— JOHN KOTTER AND DAN COHEN[9]

DON'T BE INVISIBLE

If we can't literally build walls around groups of 150 people, how do we foster this sense of community and positive influence? It starts with being cognizant of when we need to merely *inform* employees and when we need to *engage* them, and how we make sure that our communications are visible, not invisible.

A report by Right Management Consultants entitled "Best Practices in Employee Communication" confirms that employees look to leaders' behavior when they are forming their own perceptions and behaviors. The report cites research by Jim Shaffer that shows:

- 55 percent of employees form perceptions on leadership based on what leaders say and do
- 30 percent of employees form perceptions on the company's processes, or what they actually experience in the workplace
- 15 percent of employees form perceptions from formal communications like the intranet, newsletters, and e-mails[11]

This research points out a couple of interesting insights. First, it becomes clear how little impact our formal communications have. Intuitively, it makes sense that what we say and do—*what we demonstrate*—has a much greater impact. But because we are so busy and fragmented, we still overrely on these formal types of communication.[12]

Second, if 55 percent of our employees' perceptions are formed based on what we demonstrate, we had better be very intentional with our actions. The report puts it in these terms: "This research illustrates the need for leadership throughout the organization to communicate and engage their employees in the business strategy, and visibly demonstrate what it looks like."[13] This is one of the unexpected surprises that comes with a leadership role—suddenly every action you take becomes very visible.

This begs the question, How do leaders "engage" employees and make strategy, performance goals, differentiation, service tactics, and the like "visible"? How do we take something that is intangible, such as delivering client delight, and make it visible?

In the very act of telling a story, we can't help but engage people. The act of telling and the act of listening build the necessary engagement to help get important information and knowledge across. And the context of the story makes the content "visible." People get to see what is normally removed in the filtering process. They get to see how certain conclusions were reached, where the struggles were, how different people reacted, and what results they got.

Most often in organizations, stories get created by individuals or small groups. They are "lived" by someone in the group, and then often shared with that person's immediate peers. If the story turns out to be inconsequential, then the story quickly dies. But if the story turns out to have a lot of value to the organization, something needs to be done with it. It needs to go beyond the immediate vicinity of the teller. This is where the biggest risk to communications occurs, because it is in that small group where even valuable stories die.

Why do these stories die? They die because they never get told beyond the small group. Or, even if they are recognized as valuable, they are broken into pieces and parsed to fit into convenient boxes shaped by our existing channels—newsletters, intranets, slides, etc. How do we ensure that the story has more reach? The most common way that organizations capture and retell these critical stories is by using a filtering process. Once a story's value has become clear, the story gets parsed into its informational components and put in a variety of places. Pieces of the story—the key lessons—find their way into training materials, PowerPoint presentations, and even job descriptions.

> "The pure quantity of messages that go out to employees necessitates better manager communication to filter and emphasize the messages that are important."
>
> — JIM SHAFER[14]

There exist many filters in our businesses, from human resources filters for appropriateness to legal filters designed to protect the company and our own self-imposed filters of time and creativity. As in Figure 3.2, lack of time and creativity cause us to strip away the most important content and context from what we are trying to communicate. For challenges that affect large groups, communications go through additional filters (most often HR and legal/compliance) that strip away even more context to make the communications broadly relevant. But, at this point, what's left is useless, and will not impact or change behavior.

The problem with this filtering process is that once a story goes through it, the value has been almost completely removed from the story and the lessons are very hard to discern. One of the issues

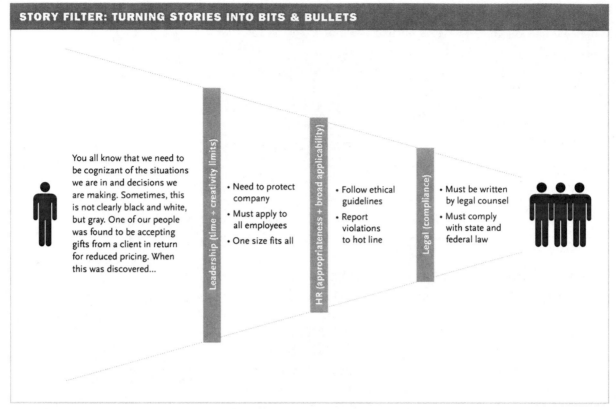

STORY FILTER: TURNING STORIES INTO BITS & BULLETS

You all know that we need to be cognizant of the situations we are in and decisions we are making. Sometimes, this is not clearly black and white, but gray. One of our people was found to be accepting gifts from a client in return for reduced pricing. When this was discovered...

Leadership (time + creativity limits)
- Need to protect company
- Must apply to all employees
- One size fits all

HR (appropriateness + broad applicability)
- Follow ethical guidelines
- Report violations to hot line

Legal (compliance)
- Must be written by legal counsel
- Must comply with state and federal law

FIGURE 3.2 The Story Filter

"In the information age, there can be a temptation to over communicate. We need to have less noise and be clearer about key messages."

– JOHN EGAN[15]

that many leaders are blind to is this filtering process. Because they know the original story, they can easily understand the bits and bullets into which the story was turned, and for them, the lessons are clear. But, of course, they had the benefit of the original context and the meaning of the story. Those critical components are now gone. They have been filtered out in a well-intended attempt to save time and reach more people.

Another way to look at this problem is pictured in Figure 3.3, Putting Humpty Dumpty Back Together Again. Because we are moving so fast and the flow of information never slows, it is often very difficult to put these pieces (the context, lessons, etc.) back together. But that's just what we have to do—to make whole something that has been broken apart.

PUTTING HUMPTY DUMPTY BACK TOGETHER AGAIN

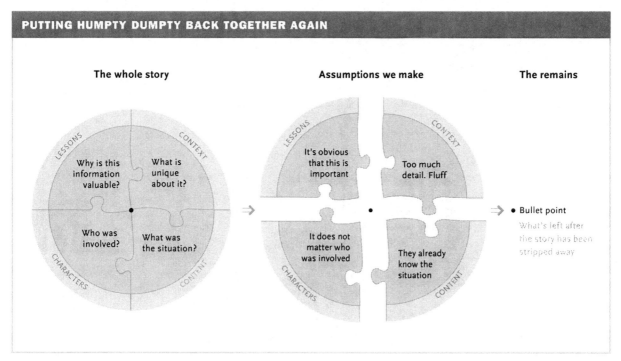

The whole story   Assumptions we make   The remains

LESSONS — Why is this information valuable?   CONTEXT — What is unique about it?

CHARACTERS — Who was involved?   CONTENT — What was the situation?

LESSONS — It's obvious that this is important   CONTEXT — Too much detail. Fluff

CHARACTERS — It does not matter who was involved   CONTENT — They already know the situation

- Bullet point

What's left after the story has been stripped away

FIGURE 3.3 Putting Humpty Dumpty Back Together Again

Often unconsciously, we strip away the most important components of a story. The lessons and context are obvious to us, so they are removed in order to get straight to the point, usually the bullet point. Instead, we must pull together the components of the story and tell it.

Figure 3.4 shows that with a little time and creativity, we can put the story back together. We can add back the critical elements (context, situation, characters) that give people an example to connect to and consider.

You might ask: That sounds good, but won't I have the same problem with reaching many people with the story? Won't the story again be restricted to those in my immediate vicinity? The answer to these questions is no, because there are a number of ways that stories can be given more reach.

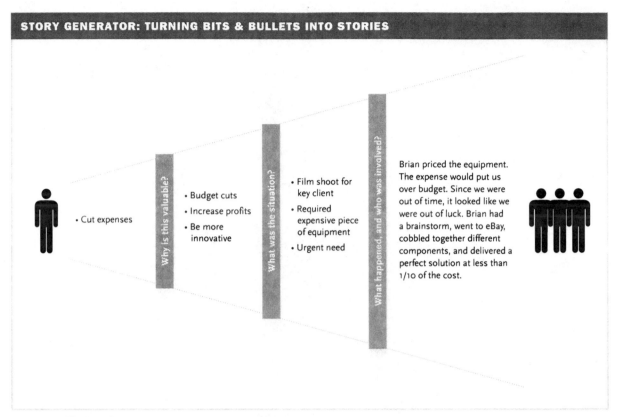

STORY GENERATOR: TURNING BITS & BULLETS INTO STORIES

Why is this valuable?
- Cut expenses
- Budget cuts
- Increase profits
- Be more innovative

What was the situation?
- Film shoot for key client
- Required expensive piece of equipment
- Urgent need

What happened, and who was involved?

Brian priced the equipment. The expense would put us over budget. Since we were out of time, it looked like we were out of luck. Brian had a brainstorm, went to eBay, cobbled together different components, and delivered a perfect solution at less than 1/10 of the cost.

FIGURE 3.4 The Story Generator

THE KEY INGREDIENT

The first, and most important, challenge in increasing the value of communications is recognizing that a story needs to be told. You have discovered that a story could have a lot of value and you have resisted the temptation to ignore it, parse it, break it into bullet points, and otherwise spindle and mutilate it. What now?

Tell it! Use the communications tools at your disposal to tell the story. A story is a tool that can be highly leveraged because it "costs" little but has a powerful impact. Stories told by leaders can be used in conjunction with each of the communications methods listed above, making those tools much more valuable.

Many leaders have told me that, thanks to recognizing the stories all around them, they are running their meetings and confer-

STORYSCAPE

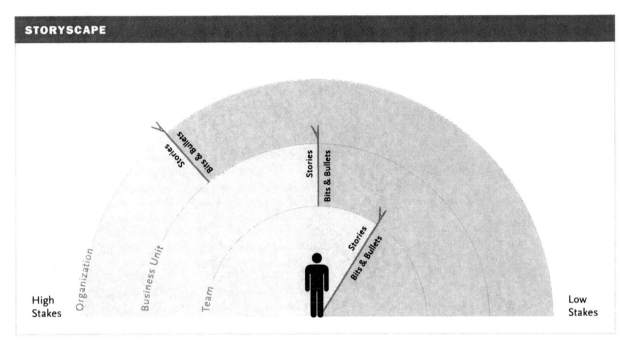

FIGURE 3.5 Storyscape

ences much differently. In the past, as they sat down to prepare for employee conferences and important meetings, they simply pulled together what they wanted to communicate into slides and then presented those slides, with predictable results.

Depending on our organization and whom we serve, we must choose the right combination of stories and bits and bullets for each audience—immediate face-to-face colleagues, a business unit or dispersed team, and the greater organization. Striking the right balance between stories and bits and bullets depends on the stakes involved, and thus we must constantly adjust the levers shown in Figure 3.5 to find the appropriate balance.

Because they are more conscious of the impact of their stories, they choose stories to illustrate key insights and behaviors that people need to demonstrate. They turn these routine meetings and conferences into opportunities to enhance the performance of their people (and themselves) and not just settle for (expensive) data-sharing sessions.

CLASH OF CULTURES

A client of mine who is a senior leader in charge of about 8,000 people told me this story.

His organization was entertaining a merger with another large corporation. The merger looked great on paper and the economics made sense. So, inevitably, the two senior teams had to come together to discuss the sticky subject of how the leadership structure would work. My client is known for his collaborative style of management and thus his senior team was collegial and worked as a tight group that lacked hierarchical structure.

The other company, however, was run by the former governor of the state, and was a very hierarchical company. What the governor said was what was done, nothing more and nothing less. His was a command-and-control style and when the two teams got together, no one talked but the governor. He was to be called "Governor."

When the groups came to together to evaluate the real possibility of joining forces, the two teams mixed like oil and water, and it didn't take long to establish that these two leadership teams would have a very hard time integrating into one entity. It took only one meeting to figure out that this merger was dead on arrival. My client and his team walked away and, subsequently, went on to merge successfully several times with more compatible teams (and they continue to do so today) and have created a large, successful enterprise.

My client told me this story right after he had told it to 300 people in his organization, 50 of whom were part of a newly acquired company. He said he could have just put "Collaborative Management Styles Work Best" on a slide, and called it a day. But he wanted the new folks to really understand that he put his money where his mouth is!

Similarly, stories can be infused into other communications tools as well. The company intranet, newsletter, and other blanket communications can tell short stories in written form that, for all of the reasons outlined in Chapter 2, will be more sticky and thus have more impact. A story of the week or featured story on the intranet will get more eyeball time than the section on last quarter's news.

Some organizations are also starting to use stories in their learning efforts as well. Traditional tools like classroom-based training and relatively new tools like Webinars, virtual classrooms, and Web-based scenarios (this is what my company designs and builds) are increasingly finding room to share stories. Stories are infusing these tools in order to *put the context back on the performance goals.* Instead of fancy "virtual" PowerPoint slides or linear e-learning, many organizations are asking their employees to participate in a rich story, collaborate around what's happening in the story, and, thereby, truly understand what success and failure look like.

"Over thousands of years, we have learned the practice of sharing stories and creating narratives in face-to-face encounters. But if storytelling remains anchored in this face-to-face domain, it may be limited value for geographically dispersed organizations. In effect, we may be missing the potential of technology to stretch the scope and scale of the benefits of practice, narrative, and storytelling."

— JOHN SEELY BROWN[16]

STOP BEING A "PETE"!

Several years ago, WisdomTools created a story for a large technology and services client of ours that wanted its product development people (a group of about 1,200) to have a deeper understanding of the process by which products came to market. So we created a story about a fictional group of people at this company from different levels of management struggling with getting a new product through the pipeline. One of the characters we developed, Pete, was an especially difficult person who liked to boss others around and generally be a pain in the neck. When the story was completed and the Web-based scenario began to unfold throughout the company, Pete became infamous. People in meetings would say to each other, "You are being a 'Pete.' Stop it!" When we heard this, we knew we had helped to create a story that was sticky and that would live on to influence people's behavior in a positive way.

These organizations have realized that a good story gets told and retold and people gain meaning with each pass. Bits and bullets can get you to first base, but they won't bring you all the way home.

A handful of organizations have even produced books about their past that serve as a communications tool for new employees and as a way to connect them to the culture. These books are a great way to understand where a company came from, the early successes, and what makes the company unique.

Even good old voicemail can be used as a vehicle for delivering stories. The former CEO of the Forum Corporation used to leave company-wide voicemails that would begin with something like: "It's a crisp and snowy day here in Boston, and the streets and sidewalks are white, as if preparing for the holidays. I rose out of bed today thinking of all of you and how much we've accomplished..." For an entire day after one of these famous voicemails, the organization would be laughing and discussing "John's latest message," but what was really happening was that the company's strong and tight-knit culture was being reinforced—in real time (then there was the day when John left a message about his turkey-stuffing recipe!).

Organizations that have begun to infuse stories into their communications more consistently and intentionally have discovered an antidote to story deficit disorder. They find themselves cutting through the noise, giving people something they can bite into, and building stronger connections. And they are having a lot more fun. If we begin to be more discerning about which of our communications are high stakes and which are not, then we can be more consistent and intentional about telling the right stories at the right time. The next step is learning how to capture those stories in the first place!

"The idea of learning as the steady supply of facts or information, though parodied by Dickens 150 years ago, still prevails today. Each generation has its own fight against images of learners as wax to be modeled, pitchers to be filled, and slates to be written on."

– JOHN SEELY BROWN AND PAUL DUGUID[17]

SUMMARY

THE BITS AND BULLETS

- There is a big difference between high-stakes and low-stakes communications, and we must be more discerning about which tools we are using in which situations.

- Just stop and reflect on your own use of bits and bullets and stories. Are you in balance? Are you giving people the how and why and not just the what?

- Be aware of the filters that information goes through before it gets to people. Is it still powerful when it gets to them?

- Step into the void and engage people with a story.

- Some organizations are beginning to be more conscious of their use of stories, and they are creating innovative ways of cutting through the clutter to offer people stories that drive results.

THE PICTURES

High-Stakes versus Low-Stakes Communications
We can't treat all communications the same way

The Story Filter
How bullet points get created almost by default

Putting Humpty Dumpty Back Together Again
Stories put the context and color back on the facts

The Story Generator
Reverse the filters, and people will get more of what they need to perform

Storyscape
What is your storyscape? Adjust your "levers" and give people more stories

THE STORIES

You Know You Are Abusing Bits and Bullets When...
Learning to recognize the signs

Everything's "Awesome"!
Becoming cognizant of how people are receiving the messages

Clash of Cultures
Building a strong culture through stories

Stop Being a "Pete"!
Stories have a much broader impact on performance by taking on a life of their own

CHAPTER 3:
MY THOUGHTS AND IDEAS

PART THREE

A solution is useless without a good implementation plan. The first real lesson I learned in business was *don't come to me with problems; come to me with solutions.* This forced me not only to think through a good solution, but also to be darn sure I could put it into action. In that spirit, I have created the following story tools to help leaders put their stories into action.

Chapter 4 discusses the first story tool, the Win Book. Leaders need a place to capture what's happening all around them. Invariably, we come across many art facts, situations, and stories as we move through our very busy lives. The Win Book provides a central place to write down these experiences and reflect on them. One of the things that is critical to successful leadership is that when we do find those rare few minutes to reflect and plan, we have a resource that is truly designed for us with the information and context that is relevant to our particular situation.

In Chapter 5, we look to another story tool, the Story Matrix, to turn the context and insights of the Win Book into stories that we can readily access. The Story Matrix is our personal story "library," complete with our stories and experiences that tell people who we are, what we care about, and how we can help them (and ourselves) perform better.

The last story tool is the Story Coach. In Chapter 6, we look at how to turn these stories into action. Once we have a story to tell, the Story Coach looks at how to tell that story in such a way that we positively impact the people we are trying to reach. Just as a good sports coach helps shape our actions and behaviors on the field, the Story Coach gives us some parameters within which to engage and perform.

As with any contact sport, sharing stories requires discipline and practice!

CHAPTER 4:

THE WIN BOOK

EMBARRASSMENT OF RICHES

We all have hundreds or even thousands of stories in our "mental archive." And more stories are piling up all the time. In fact, there are so many stories unfolding all around us, it's an embarrassment of riches. But just like the last 20 jokes you've heard, it's nearly impossible to remember your stories when you need them.

We've all met natural storytellers. Like natural joke tellers, who can remember every joke they've ever heard, natural storytellers always seem to have a story that fits—a story that illustrates the point perfectly. I'm very lucky to have a mentor like this. He can remember the perfect story to tell me when I'm struggling with a work challenge, or a funny story when he senses that I just need to lighten up a bit. But what can the rest of us do? How can we remember the stories that will help us ignite performance, be more successful, and have more fun? How do we interpret what's happening around us into stories and how can we keep this house of stories in some semblance of order?

The personal productivity industry is huge and growing. Companies like Franklin Covey, Palm, and others are constantly innovating products and services that help us get organized, manage our time and commitments, and get the most out of every day. These products are very valuable because they help us deal with the rush of business and of life.

"To be an impact player in business, you simply have to know more than most other people know. That means taking the power of ideas seriously, reading books voraciously, and developing a system of organizing what you've learned."
— TIM SANDERS[1]

Another burgeoning industry—called the fastest growing industry in the world recently by the television show *20/20*—is the
scrapbooking business. People are spending more money on photos, books, and materials to create keepsakes for their friends and
families. Why has growth in this industry exploded? Do we now
have more memories? Do we have more data and pictures to keep
track of than before? Maybe. But I think it has more to do with
trying to get our arms around the pace of life. Scrapbooking is
growing because we are hungry for experiences that ground us
and pull us together.

The devices we carry around mostly help us manage the bits
and bullets of life—our appointments; the dates and times of events;
names and addresses; passwords; and notes. But what can we do to
manage and organize our stories? A device didn't exist—until now.

> "To change an organization, you have to change its stories."
>
> – RICHARD STONE[2]

The Win Book approach grew out of my desire *not to forget*
the important ideas, events, and stories of my life and work. After
spending a considerable amount of time researching (and using)
many different paper-based and electronic tools, I found none that
provided that "pan" that I could use to sift for gold.

You may be wondering why it's called a Win Book if it captures
all stories, including failure stories. Simply, it's because if you've captured failures and learned from them, you've turned them into wins.

In developing the Win Book approach, I was attempting to capture facts, ideas, and concepts that would make me a better leader,
planner, and person. The Win Book concept has a lot in common
with a scrapbook, but it is a business tool. Whereas a typical scrapbook is concerned with memories and keepsakes, a Win Book is focused on capturing business information in such a way that the information can be turned into stories to increase performance.

WIN "FILE" TO WIN "BOOK"

Fifteen years ago, I became aware of the concept of a win "file"
while selling for IBM. The concept is a very simple one that takes
much of what we know about how adults learn and combines it
into a powerful tool for leaders.

When I first learned of the win file, it was simply a plain old ma-
nila file folder in which a person would keep all positive feedback
he or she had received. The basic idea was that if someone wrote a
note or an e-mail describing the great job you had done providing

service to a large client, you copied the note or printed the e-mail and put it in your win file. If you received a strong performance review, you copied it and put it in the file. That way, whenever you needed some motivation or inspiration, the file was there. It was not generic. It was not a motivational poster with a soaring eagle on the wall; it was about *you*. You could revisit the successes you had and be reminded of how you had achieved those results.

Because adults need large doses of both action *and* reflection in order to learn, this win file idea had a lot going for it. I was so taken by this concept that I spent the next 15 years adding to and refining the idea of the win file, and it has been a powerful resource for me in my own learning journey.

Over time, the "file" morphed into a series of composition books (those black and white speckled notebooks that now accompany your nightmares about writing school exams). Each book had its own distinct subject, such as "Client: DaimlerChrysler" or "New Products." As the scope of my responsibilities slowly expanded, some books were titled "Operations," "Strategic Planning," and even "People." In each book, I captured notes and ideas about that particular subject as it unfolded. Over a couple of years, I had so many books on so many different clients and subjects that the system became unwieldy, and that precipitated the next stage of evolution.

This next stage of evolution for the Win Book concept—and the most current iteration—saw the Win Book morph again from the small composition books into a more robust, lined, and bound book that has much more staying power. Because the book is bigger and of better quality, I now capture all subjects in chronological order and I can move quickly and easily between different subjects. The Win Book has turned into a very valuable and powerful business tool.

I use my Win Book as a book about my life, not just my work, and it has elements of everything that is important to me. It serves as a repository of my experiences that remind me of the important moments and stories of my life. It never fails to bring a smile to my face as I look back a couple of months or a couple of years and recall what was happening at the time—sales strategies that brought success, a funny note from a colleague, a picture from vacation, or a great e-mail from a client.

"The last few decades have belonged to a certain kind of person with a certain kind of mind—computer programmers who could crank code, lawyers who could craft contracts, MBAs who could crunch numbers. But the keys to the kingdom are changing hands. The future belongs to a very different kind of mind—creators and empathizers, pattern recognizers, and meaning makers. The people—artists, inventors, designers, storytellers, caregivers, consolers, big picture thinkers—will now reap society's richest rewards and share its greatest joys."

— Daniel Pink[3]

"You may think you know, but you don't
know until you write it down."

– ROBERT McKEE[4]

My Win Book grew from a repository where I captured work-related artifacts and ideas to a place where I could capture and reflect on all the different experiences of my life. This step in the evolution of the book was influenced by watching my wife Jill use small journals to capture our kids' funny sayings, first experiences, and pictures.

ELEMENTS OF THE WIN BOOK

The Win Book takes organization to the next level and turns the experiences and artifacts of your life into your personal competitive advantage. Your Win Book can take shape as a file, a notebook, a day planner, a daily journal and scrapbook (like mine), or any number of different forms; the key is finding the form that is most useful for you. It's not important that you use it exactly as I describe here. What's most important is that the Win Book provides an *unedited* central archive of your successes, failures, thoughts, and conversations as they occur, and concepts that need to be *acted* upon. The Win Book is not the place for editing and judging—if it strikes you, include it.

The Win Book is not just a mechanism to help us reflect on what's important, it is a device to spur us to action—well-informed action that is directed and focused.

As a tool for leaders, the Win Book is a flexible solution that combines a number of elements. It can include any combination of the following elements:

• A central archive of daily conversations, meetings, and presentations
• To-do lists
• Notes about employees, their successes and failures, and needs for development
• Client meetings, notes, and associated action items
• Marketing ideas and action plans
• Articles, clips, or pictures that need to be remembered or put to immediate use
• Illustrations and models that apply to your business challenges
• Ideas, thoughts, and plans regarding your work and life
• Stories and news clippings that you find interesting or impact you in some way
• A simple index of what is contained in the book

Your Win Book does not have to include all of these things. Some leaders who have adopted this concept use it only for capturing insights and feedback about their direct reports. Some use it only as a book into which to write notes during meetings. Some leaders have adapted the concept and used it as a gift to their people by creating Win Books for each of their employees with notes and clippings about why that person is a strong contributor.

As Figure 4.1 shows, we collect stories everywhere. Depending on your personal style, some of these stories may be appropriate to capture in your Win Book.

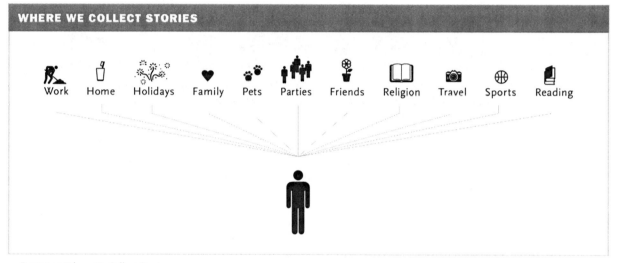

FIGURE 4.1 Where We Collect Stories

The Win Book brings together your to-dos, articles you find interesting, coaching and feedback moments, meeting notes, conversations with clients, funny things your kids said, and anything else you want to capture during the course of your work.

All of these elements are written down, or simply printed or copied and pasted into the book. Once you fill up a book, start a new one. The tool is very flexible, and everyone has different ideas about what their book will contain based on what's important to them.

In order for a Win Book to become a tool for leaders, it must become a central place where great ideas are stored and where things such as employee recognition and stories that have impacted you

"Information has perfectly increasing returns. Spend the money to learn something once, and that knowledge can be reused at zero additional cost forever. Double the number of uses and the cost per unit halves."

— PHILIP EVANS AND THOMAS WURSTER[5]

and the business are captured *as they are unfolding.* The Win Book should capture thoughts you've had about what you have read and learned. It should be a place where you write down how a project became successful or why you lost a competitive proposal. When the Win Book contains these elements, it truly becomes a resource that you can use to take action on your business and your life.

USING YOUR WIN BOOK

There are many different ways to use the Win Book. In the pages that follow, several examples will illustrate the different types of information captured in a Win Book, and how some of that information becomes stories. See Figures 4.2–4.6

Reflection, Context, and a Place to Organize Things

As I hope you saw in these examples, the Win Book encompasses three critical elements of learning and leadership: reflection, context, and a place to organize things. When you carry with you a tool like the Win Book, sitting on a flight or waiting for a meeting becomes an opportunity to reflect on the prior month and pour over ideas that you haven't had time to consider. You may come across a bit of positive feedback that could be used again or a fact that would be very helpful to a client. Win Book artifacts that are meaningful to your life and business have continued relevance long after they would have been forgotten had they been tossed in the back of a file cabinet or placed in a photo album.

Most leaders read business books, thereby "reflecting" on what's important for their business. Reading "voraciously," as Tim Sanders puts it, is extremely important to gather new ideas or different ways to think about our challenges. When you *transfer* your learning from a business book into your Win Book, it becomes *your* knowledge. Your Win Book quickly becomes the business book that is written *by* you, *for* you, and *about* you. In this way, there is much less distance between the ideas and your ability to implement and take action on them.

The nuts and bolts of organizing your life—your file cabinet, BlackBerry, phone, car visor, kitchen table, etc.—record your to-dos, contacts, and information, but they don't provide context. Context is created when we see how things relate to each other, either in patterns or in time. Because the Win Book is chronologi-

> "Unlike numbers, experiences are irrefutable. You can't second-guess your experiences."
>
> – GUNNAR NILSSON[6]

cal, it serves a powerful function that devices, such as a BlackBerry, don't; it puts your ideas and events in context. The Win Book recaps conversations you have had with employees and clients *at a point in time*, and also captures what else was driving your attention during this time. The benefit of this structure is that it gives you a sense not only for how things are happening in time, but how they might have been influenced by other events that were unfolding at the same time. This adds context that is usually lost when each artifact or conversation is parsed, filed, and forgotten.

FINDING THE EDGES OF THE PUZZLE

Remember the last time you did a jigsaw puzzle? What's the key to putting it together? Finding the edges. The edges serve as the outline, or context, of the puzzle. If you can get the edges assembled—the boundaries within which to organize the rest of your efforts—filling in the rest of the puzzle becomes a whole lot easier.

A Win Book can help you find the edges of the puzzle. Say your challenge is to motivate a seasoned employee who is struggling through a low point. Look through the interactions with this person in your Win Books, collecting any insights, patterns, or artifacts that form the "edges" of the puzzle. You may find some project successes to which he contributed, some frustrations he shared with you, and some notes from colleagues who had great things to say about him. You may find an idea he shared with you a while back that turned out to have a lot of value.

Sitting down with this employee, going over these items, and reminding him of these otherwise forgotten contributions will bring him back to what excites him about the business and how meaningful his contributions have been. This interaction, based on real artifacts from your Win Books, will help to motivate him to create even more of these successes, because you've helped him make sense of the puzzle.

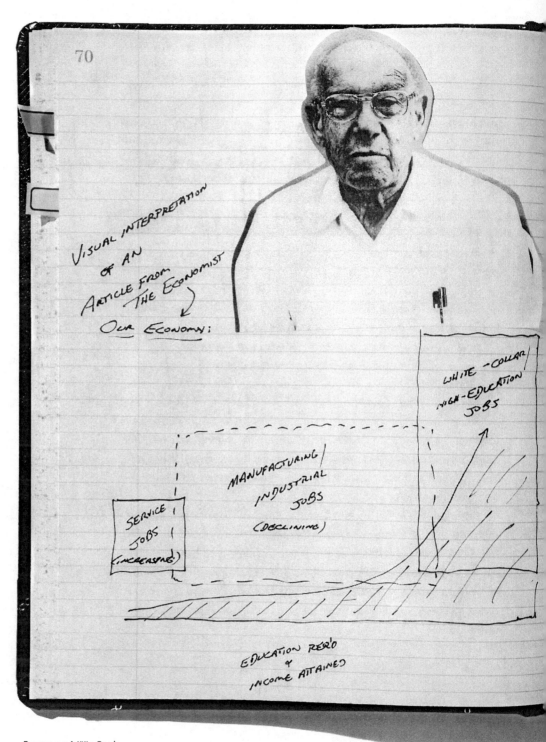

FIGURE 4.2 A Win Book

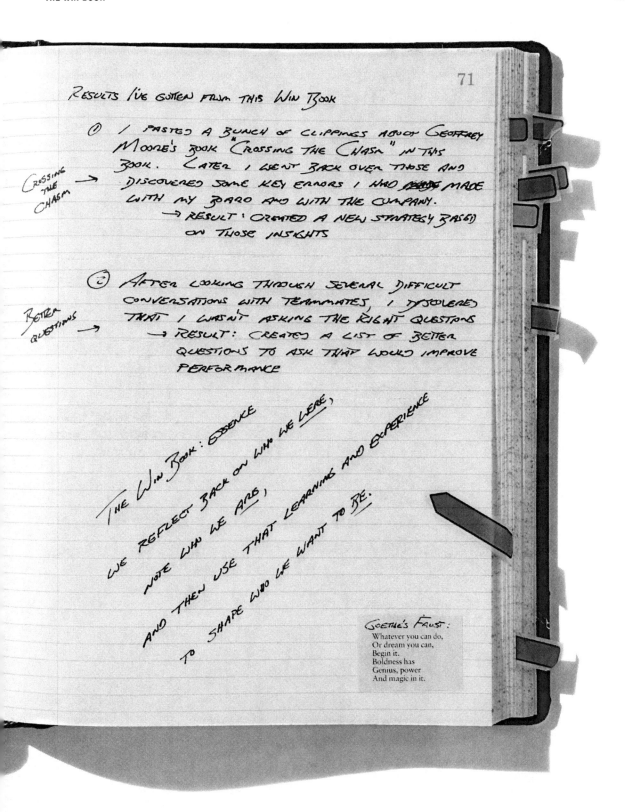

71

RESULTS I'VE GOTTEN FROM THIS WIN BOOK

① I PASTED A BUNCH OF CLIPPINGS ABOUT GEOFFREY MOORE'S BOOK "CROSSING THE CHASM" IN THIS BOOK. LATER I WENT BACK OVER THOSE AND DISCOVERED SOME KEY ERRORS I HAD MADE WITH MY BOARD AND WITH THE COMPANY.

Crossing the Chasm →

→ RESULT: CREATED A NEW STRATEGY BASED ON THOSE INSIGHTS

② AFTER LOOKING THROUGH SEVERAL DIFFICULT CONVERSATIONS WITH TEAMMATES, I DISCOVERED THAT I WASN'T ASKING THE RIGHT QUESTIONS

Better questions →

→ RESULT: CREATED A LIST OF BETTER QUESTIONS TO ASK THAT WOULD IMPROVE PERFORMANCE

THE WIN BOOK: ESSENCE
WE REFLECT BACK ON WHO WE WERE,
NOTE WHO WE ARE,
AND THEN USE THAT LEARNING AND EXPERIENCE
TO SHAPE WHO WE WANT TO BE.

GOETHE'S FAUST:
Whatever you can do,
Or dream you can,
Begin it.
Boldness has
Genius, power
And magic in it.

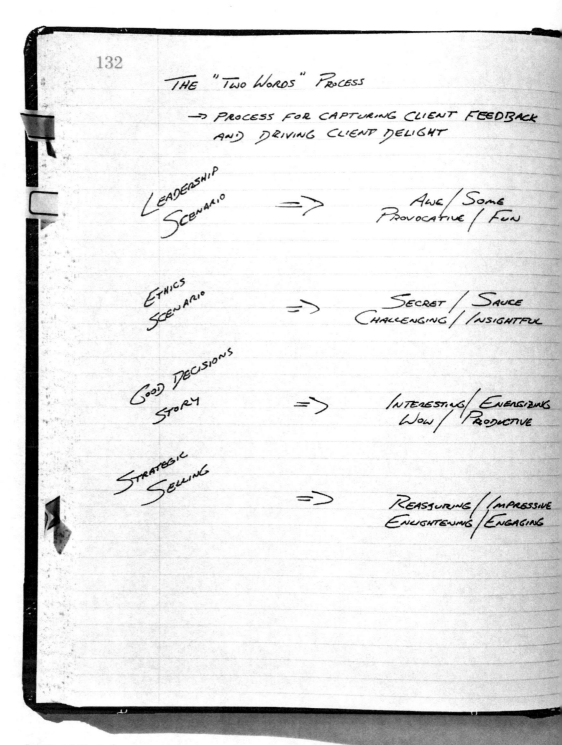

Figure 4.3 A Win Book

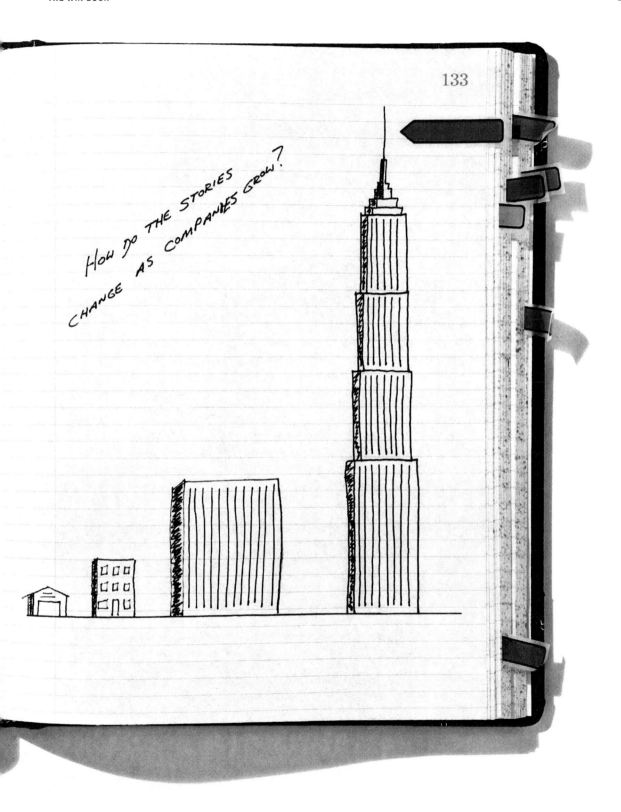

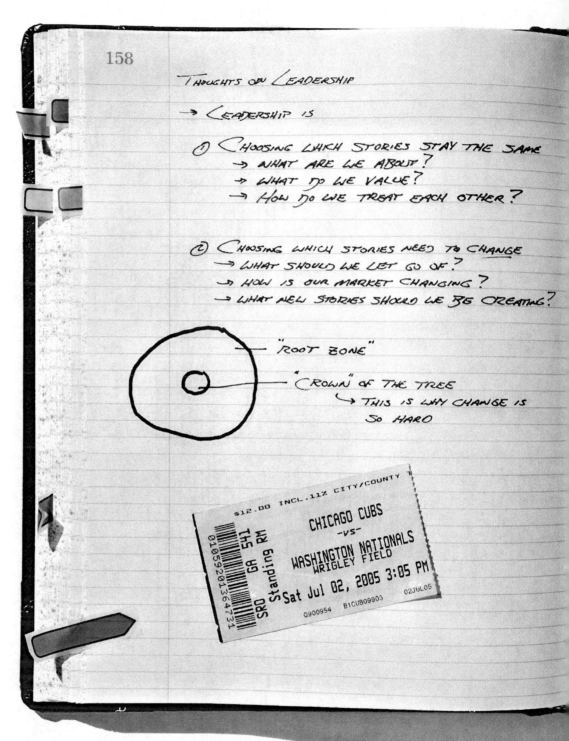

FIGURE 4.4 A Win Book

159

METAPHOR FOR LEADERSHIP & ORGANIZATIONS

LEAVES ⟹ LOW-STAKES
SHIFTING, SMALL STUFF

BRANCHES ⟹ HIGH-STAKES
BIG GOALS, OBJECTIVES

ROOTS ⟹ CORE VALUES
UNCHANGING

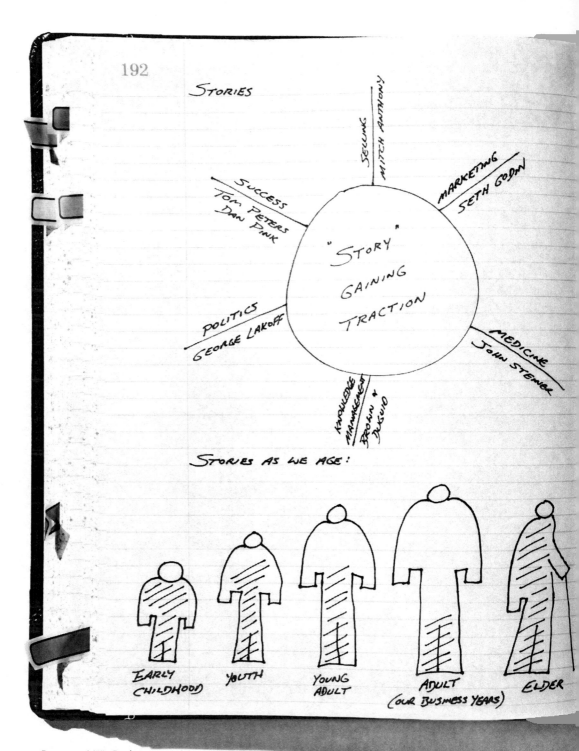

FIGURE 4.5 A Win Book

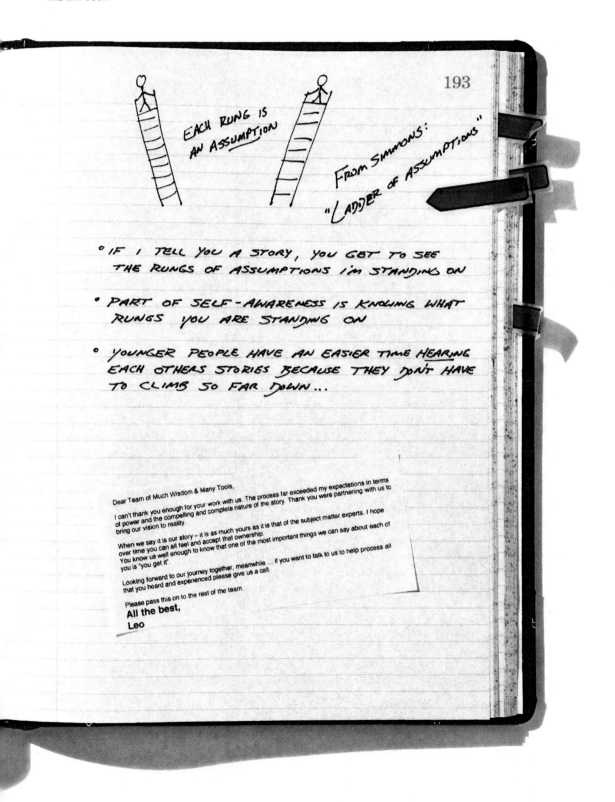

193

EACH RUNG IS
AN ASSUMPTION

FROM SIMMONS:
"LADDER OF ASSUMPTIONS"

° IF I TELL YOU A STORY, YOU GET TO SEE
THE RUNGS OF ASSUMPTIONS I'M STANDING ON

° PART OF SELF-AWARENESS IS KNOWING WHAT
RUNGS YOU ARE STANDING ON

° YOUNGER PEOPLE HAVE AN EASIER TIME HEARING
EACH OTHERS STORIES BECAUSE THEY DON'T HAVE
TO CLIMB SO FAR DOWN...

Dear Team of Much Wisdom & Many Tools,

I can't thank you enough for your work with us. The process far exceeded my expectations in terms
of power and the compelling and complete nature of the story. Thank you were partnering with us to
bring our vision to reality.

When we say it is our story – it is as much yours as it is that of the subject matter experts. I hope
over time you can all feel and accept that ownership.
You know us well enough to know that one of the most important things we can say about each of
you is "you get it".

Looking forward to our journey together, meanwhile ... if you want to talk to us to help process all
that you heard and experienced please give us a call.

Please pass this on to the rest of the team.

All the best,

Leo

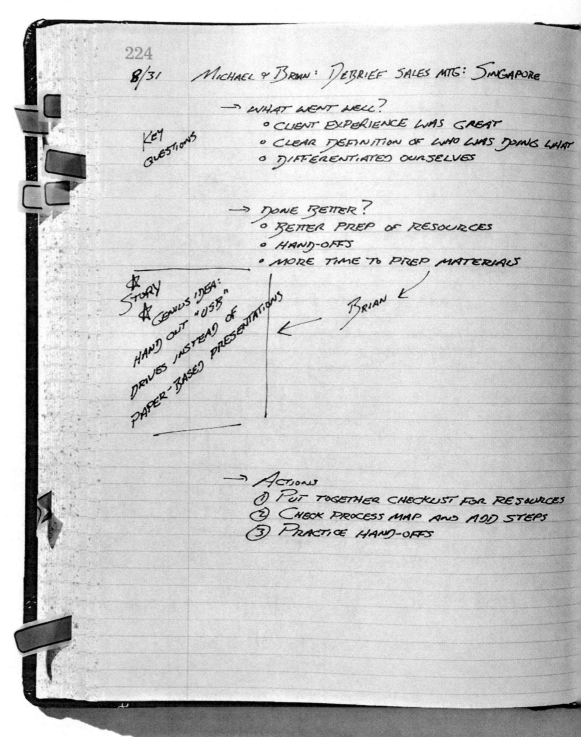

224

8/31   Michael & Brian: Debrief Sales Mtg: Singapore

→ What Went Well?
  ○ Client Experience Was Great
  ○ Clear Definition of Who Was Doing What
  ○ Differentiated Ourselves

Key Questions

→ Done Better?
  ○ Better Prep of Resources
  ○ Hand-Offs
  ○ More Time to Prep Materials

Story   Genius Idea:
Hand Out "USB" Drives Instead of Paper-Based Presentations

Brian

→ Actions
  ① Put Together Checklist for Resources
  ② Check Process Map and Add Steps
  ③ Practice Hand-Offs

FIGURE 4.6 A Win Book

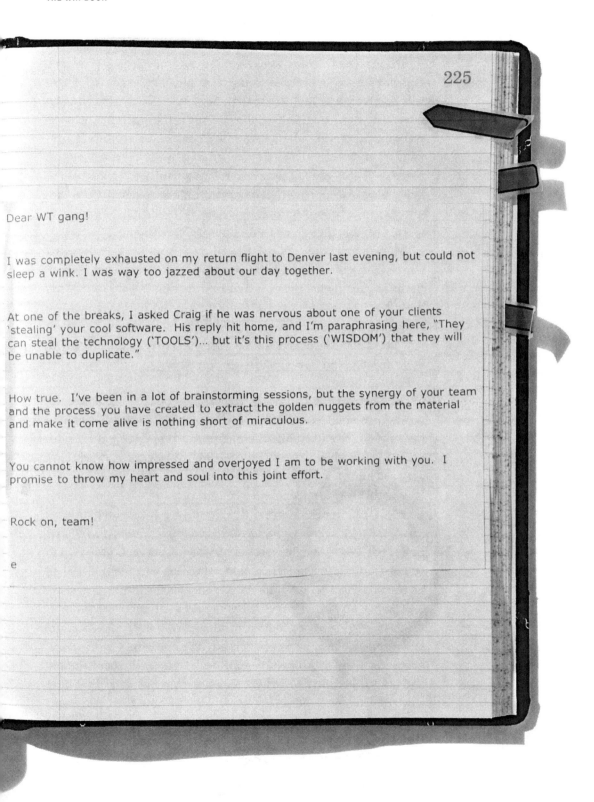

225

Dear WT gang!

I was completely exhausted on my return flight to Denver last evening, but could not sleep a wink. I was way too jazzed about our day together.

At one of the breaks, I asked Craig if he was nervous about one of your clients 'stealing' your cool software. His reply hit home, and I'm paraphrasing here, "They can steal the technology ('TOOLS')... but it's this process ('WISDOM') that they will be unable to duplicate."

How true. I've been in a lot of brainstorming sessions, but the synergy of your team and the process you have created to extract the golden nuggets from the material and make it come alive is nothing short of miraculous.

You cannot know how impressed and overjoyed I am to be working with you. I promise to throw my heart and soul into this joint effort.

Rock on, team!

e

Your Win Book shows you where you've been, who you've talked to, and what you've seen. You can look at an entry in your Win Book and quickly recall what was going on around this event. What else was happening in your life at that moment? Where were you and what else were you thinking about? This is the stuff that helps us recognize patterns, whether they are positive or negative. Unrelated facts, dates, and models are useless to us if they are not set in context—if they are not placed in relation to other things that are happening to us or to decisions we must make. When patterns begin to emerge from seemingly unrelated facts and data, we begin to learn, and only then can we take appropriate action.

More importantly, as you flip through your Win Book, what you have discovered and what you have learned becomes clearer. Because you "mine" the data and information in your Win Book with a different focus than when you captured it, things that you weren't able to see before come to light. The mind-set you had when you jotted down a conversation with a client may be long gone two months later, and now you can see something to which you were previously blind.

Similarly, combing through your Win Book is also learning. As you reflect on notes and ideas that you captured weeks or months before, you are embedding these ideas, and combining them with other ideas and situations. This provides the spark that precedes action. This is learning.

Another way to understand what you've learned is to understand which of your opinions have shifted over time. In combing through my Win Books, I often come across old conversations and strategies that at the time I thought were very powerful, but that turned out to be noise. It is in this process of understanding why those ideas had no traction that I become more discerning for the future.

Having a place to organize your ideas is not as trivial as it sounds. Looking back six months in your Win Book and recalling client and employee conversations is a very powerful way to understand exactly why things have gone well, what tactics have worked and not worked, and how client situations have progressed. I have surprised many clients with knowledge of how their situations have changed over time. With simple file folders that are housed at the office, we rarely access interesting conversations in which value may have been hidden. Have you ever moved your office across

"Discovering new stories and telling stories on a daily basis, once a habit, builds wisdom that cannot be gained from a book, a mentor, or any other secondhand form of learning."

– ANNETTE SIMMONS[7]

the hall or across town and wondered, Where did I get all of these files, and...where's the dumpster?

In fact, the ideas and concepts for this book came from my Win Books. As I had ideas that shaped my thinking around stories, or came across interesting arguments that shed light on one of the ideas, they were all captured in my past and present Win Books. *In a very real way, Win Books filter what's important from what's not important.*

WHAT A WIN BOOK IS NOT

A Win Book is not a file cabinet. All of us have reams of loose paper comprised of contracts, employee files, handbooks, policies, and many, many others forms of information. That's why we have file cabinets. The Win Book is designed to be the central repository of what's transpiring at work (and, if you so choose, in your life) and important ideas about which you should be thinking.

> "...for seeking and learning are in fact nothing but recollection."
>
> – PLATO[8]

A Win Book is not a diary in which you pour your heart out. Just as you wouldn't try to stuff all of the random loose papers of your daily life into your bound Win Book, you should not use this tool as a place to unload all of your deepest, darkest secrets. Although the structure is there to support that type of use, the Win Book is not designed for this purpose and as a tool for leaders it would quickly become unwieldy.

Finally, a Win Book is not meant to replace your BlackBerry. It's not a calendar, e-mail device, or database. A Win Book *finds the connections and patterns* between all of this otherwise disconnected information, and is the engine that generates the stories that result from all of this activity. A Win Book generates the fuel from the raw materials you supply.

A Win Book, used consistently and deliberately, quickly becomes indispensable. Remember when you first started using a day planner and you put everything it, from your meeting schedule and address book to your favorite quotes and key phone numbers? If you lost it, even temporarily, you wanted to crawl into a hole. This same usefulness accompanies a well-constructed Win Book, because it contains everything you deem important about your business and your experiences. If your day planner or Black Berry provides the liner notes and score of your business life, then the Win Book is the music.

CHAPTER 4:
SUMMARY

THE BITS AND BULLETS

- We are moving ever faster, so use your Win Book to capture what is happening around you.

- Make your Win Book work for you because it is a business tool that you can customize according to the way you work and the information you need.

- Don't edit the material in your Win Book; just capture it without expressing an opinion.

- Over a period of time, the Win Book artifacts and ideas become valuable resources for leadership and higher performance.

- A Win Book is the "pan" that holds both the mud and grit (facts and data) and the gold (stories).

THE PICTURES

Where We Collect Stories
Everywhere!

Win Book Samples

THE STORIES

Finding the Edges of the Puzzle
A Win Book helps frame ideas and artifacts in a way that creates insights

Chapter 4:
MY THOUGHTS AND IDEAS

CHAPTER 5:

THE STORY MATRIX

"Our intelligence is enhanced by the number of stories we know and the quality of indexing we attach to those stories."

– ANNETTE SIMMONS[1]

PANNING FOR GOLD

The second tool in our toolbox is the Story Matrix. The Story Matrix is very simple. If the Win Book is the filter of your business life, then the Story Matrix is the gold that remains when the mud and grit fall through the bottom of that filter. The purpose of the Story Matrix is to give leaders ready access to their own stories so that they can be more consistent and intentional about weaving those stories into their communications. Here the connection is made—connecting desired outcomes to the stories that will help shape behavior and action.

Think of the brain as a storage room. We are constantly accumulating information and knowledge, putting it in boxes, and throwing these boxes into our storage room. Because so much information is coming at us in a never-ending wave, we just prop the door open and throw stuff in as fast as we can.

But look at the room. It's a mess! The boxes are lying all over the place and they are piled up near the entrance. Because they haven't been consistently well organized or even labeled, we have no idea where to find anything, and we are not using the space wisely. Boxes are piled up inside the doorway and the back of the room is nearly empty. We have to step over all of the boxes of junk in the doorway just to get to the stuff we really need.

Along comes the Story Matrix, which serves as the shelving, labels, and containers for your information and knowledge—your stories. It is the organizing element that makes our knowledge and information accessible and useable.

It's one thing to have a repository of stories; it's quite another to have them organized so that they become useful. Think of some of the other artifacts of your life, such as your music collection or those photos you took on your last vacation. These are very useful to you only *if* you can find what you are looking for when you need it!

The Story Matrix represents the turning point where our stories become tools to tackle our challenges and ignite performance. We have captured the stories in our Win Book, and now we must think deliberately about where a specific story will have the strongest positive impact.

> "The age-old practice of storytelling is one of the most effective tools leaders can use. But they need to pick their stories carefully and match them to the situation."
>
> – STEPHEN DENNING[2]

The Story Matrix is a simple spreadsheet that places a leader's stories into different categories, as in Figure 5.1. The stories themselves come from the Win Book (and other places) and they spread out like batter onto the waffle iron of the Story Matrix. Day by day, as you use your Win Book or comb through past win books, stories become apparent and are captured on the Story Matrix. Now, in retrospect, information and events that looked like only data points at the time they were happening become key puzzle pieces of a larger story.

STORY MATRIX

		Leadership Performance Skills					
		Culture/ Company	Execution	Sales	Service	Teamwork	Me
Story Types	Success						
	Failure						
	Fun						
	Legends						

FIGURE 5.1 Sample Story Matrix

The grid of the Story Matrix serves as a repository for different types of stories. The horizontal axis is designed to change based on the types of challenges each leader faces. The vertical axis remains the same, and serves as a reminder to tell different types of stories to help people to see all angles of a challenge.

> "Stories play a big role in institutional memory—they are the principal means by which groups remember."
>
> – CHARLOTTE LINDE[3]

THE VERTICAL AXIS—STORY TYPES

In order to serve as a tool to organize your stories, the Story Matrix is structured as a grid with two axes. The vertical axis is where the nature of stories and the different types of impact they have on performance comes into play. Although not set in stone, the vertical axis is meant to be more rigid.

> "It's all invented anyway, so we might as well invent a story or a framework of meaning that enhances our quality of life and the lives of those around us."
>
> – ROSAMUND STONE ZANDER AND BENJAMIN ZANDER[4]

The categories of success, failure, fun, and legends are the broadest four categories that still have key distinctions between them. In order to ignite performance, leaders need to be telling all four types of stories, because each type of story has a different impact.

Success

We all adore success. Success stories, when they occur, are told and retold (especially if we were responsible for the success!). These stories are easy to remember and, often, they are captured in our knowledge management systems and promoted in our marketing materials. They feel good, but they also serve a very important role in igniting performance.

Success stories show the way. They let us inside a situation, as it's unfolding, to see the key twists and turns that ultimately proved to be the deciding factors. Instead of just telling us the result—We won the Miller business!—the story of the team coming together, working late nights, shoring up their weaknesses, and preparing a fantastic presentation lets us see the ins and outs of the success. We get to see where things could have gone wrong and where the right skills or ingenuity at the right time made a huge difference.

Success stories are the most obvious type of story that leaders need to be telling and including on this axis.

Failure

Yuck. Who likes to tell stories about failure? Why bother? Everyone knows they exist, so why not just let a sleeping dog lie? This category on the vertical axis of the Story Matrix serves a very important purpose.

"Story doesn't grab power. Story creates power. You do not need a position of formal leadership when you know the power of story."

— ANNETTE SIMMONS[5]

First, the explicit "failure" category is there to remind us that as leaders, we must capture and tell these types of stories. The worst thing we can do is sweep them under the rug and ignore them.

Second, our failure stories are not only relevant, but they will actually help us build performance by helping others avoid the traps we've fallen into ourselves. After all, if people can't picture what failure looks like, how will they know they are failing? It is too easy to overlook, or forget, failure stories, and this is a huge opportunity that is often missed to better connect with people, build trust, and enhance performance. Like success stories, failure stories let us inside a failure to see exactly what went wrong. Telling stories of failure has the same benefit as one of the most powerful and underutilized tools available to leaders—the win/loss debrief.

The win/loss debrief is simply a set of questions that are asked of a client or project team after a significant event has taken place, whether that event is a lost (or won) sale, a failed (or successful) project, etc. It is rare that a win/loss debrief doesn't offer key insights into your business or your approach, even when you've won and you think you know the reasons. Often, you learn about things you could have done even better that, if acted on, will increase your performance the next time.

After failures, the debrief serves as a postmortem that almost always turns into the client "telling you the story" of how you failed. You get to see each decision point and where you went wrong. It's not easy to hear this, but you most often end up having a much clearer idea of how to perform better and you certainly have increased the level of trust with your client. Similarly, sharing failure stories almost always has a *positive* impact on performance. Herb Kelleher, the famous former CEO of Southwest Airlines, once wrote, "Customers are like a force of nature: You can't fool them, and you ignore them at your own peril."[6] It's the same with your colleagues and peers *inside* the company. You can't fool them by telling nothing but rosy success stories. They know it's not real. So why pretend?

Third, and most important, our failure stories help us build strong bonds with our people. They demonstrate that we are human and that mistakes are acceptable. This is so obvious, but so often forgotten. Jim Collins, in his book, *Good To Great*, describes what he calls a Level 5 Leader. According to Collins, one of the key aspects to Level 5 leadership is personal humility, a trait that is decidedly rare in our "celebrity CEO" culture.[7] Telling failure stories allows leaders to share what they've learned in a way that reveals that they are indeed just as fallible as everyone else. These stories break down the artificial walls that often separate the leaders in organizations. And because this is so important, there is actually a category on the horizontal axis called "Me" stories that will be explained below.

> "The good-to-great leaders were able to strip away so much noise and clutter and just focus on the few things that would have the greatest impact."
>
> – JIM COLLINS[8]

"WHEN HAVE YOU FAILED?"

I once found myself presenting to the entire executive team of one of my clients, including the CEO. I was there to try to expand our business with this client. As I wrapped up my presentation, the CEO asked, "When have you failed?" She wanted to understand how we thought about failure and whether we learned from it. I was not prepared for that question. So I told her the truth—we had indeed made mistakes, but we had always recovered. My response was disjointed, and it was clear that I hadn't ever really thought about it. She wasn't satisfied. I needed to use a story to illustrate my answer. Without a story, it was obvious to her that I didn't really have an answer, and that was the last time I met with her. Our client relationship never expanded.

Fun

Work should be fun. Why should we spend most of our waking hours doing something that's not fun? As leaders, we sometimes treat humor as a nice distraction when it happens, when we *should* treat it as one of our core roles. The subject of humor at work gets a clinical, cursory nod in most leadership books, *if* it gets recognized at all. This is a major oversight. And it's a huge missed opportunity. We need to add humor back into its rightful position in the workplace—everywhere. Why not?

Of course, humor should be appropriate, and it should not be used to belittle anyone. I am not talking about telling dirty jokes to break the ice. I'm talking about telling your funny stories. Tell your sales team the story about the time you were presenting to a room full of people and the arrogant, overly serious, senior-most guy in

"A good story cannot be devised, it has to be distilled."

— RAYMOND CHANDLER[9]

the room had just finished telling all of his minions that ubiquitous cell phones make him crazy when your cell phone begins ringing loudly in your suit pocket. (This is a true story, and it ended badly.)

Or tell your service people about the time you called the secretary of state's office to report the *great* experience you just had at the department of motor vehicles facility and his assistant, who was so surprised someone actually had a positive experience, shouted into the phone, "OH MY GOD! Hold on! Hold on! Let me grab a piece of paper!!!" (Also a true story.)

Or tell your entire organization the story of when you were about to hang up with another senior executive after closing a large deal with his company and instead of just saying, "Goodbye. Have a good day," you temporarily lost your mind and said, "Bye-bye, sweetheart. I love you." (This is also true, but it ended well.)

There are times when the only option is to get serious. And there are times when humor is the best tool in your kit. Lighten up, laugh, and learn.

In Chapter 2, we explored why stories are so powerful and why they connect to people. Fun stories provide a double dose of all of the positive aspects of a story, simply because we not only learn from them, but they are enjoyable as well.

Legends

These are the stories you already know. These are the legends of business that are passed along through the news media. One of the positive aspects (there aren't many) of the cult of the CEO that we went through in the 1980s and '90s was the stories that we learned. Stories such as Jack Welch of GE saying, "We are going to be number one or number two in every business we serve or we are not going to be in that business"; or Herb Kelleher of Southwest Airlines riding his Harley into the company's headquarters; or Bill Gates dropping out of Harvard; or Michael Dell building PCs in his college dorm room; or, going way back, Henry Ford telling his marketing people that "you can paint the cars any color you want, as long as it's black."

These are the legends that shape the ways we do business today. We all know these stories because we've all heard them dozens of times. But that doesn't make them stale. They are legends for a reason. They have staying power because they provide shortcuts for us to perform better. The story about Jack Welch helps us make better product mix decisions. The stories about Gates and Dell inspire us to try something new. The story about Herb Kelleher reminds us to have some fun and Henry Ford reminds us to take risks (or not!).

Every leader carries these legends around. Because most of us are not trying something entirely new in business, these legends show us how others tackled these same types of challenges. Why reinvent the wheel?

THE HORIZONTAL AXIS—PERFORMANCE SKILLS

Because the Story Matrix is designed to be flexible, the categories across the horizontal axis change depending on the type of leader using the matrix and the performance skills that are most critical for that leader. A senior executive will have categories of stories that focus on motivation or execution because the scope of her responsibility is large and in inverse proportion (probably) to her grasp of specific business units or situations. A midlevel executive will have a somewhat tighter, function-specific focus with categories like "Project Management," "XYZ Client Team," or just "Teamwork." An individual contributor, such as a salesperson or consultant, will have categories like "Planning," "Execution," or "Follow-through." An entrepreneur will likely have a mix of big-picture and tightly focused categories.

One of the best ways to create your categories across the top of the Story Matrix is to ask yourself the following question: *What are the five most common functional or performance areas that I have to influence?*

The Story Matrix is organized around a leader's main responsibilities and is designed to provide ready access to the stories that will have the greatest positive impact on performance. Figure 5.2 shows a full Story Matrix for an entrepreneur (me). Because I have accountability for a whole organization, the horizontal axis contains broad categories of responsibilities versus a more specific, business-unit focus on service or operations, for example.

The Story Matrix can be focused on the past, present, or future, depending on the story. Stories are captured as they occur, so they will often have happened in the past, whether distant or very recent. But the Story Matrix also begs the question, *What kinds of stories do I want to be telling in the future?* In this way, the Story Matrix is a powerful tool to encourage the right performance moving forward.

"Most of the time, you won't be present when the people you want to influence make the decision, choose the behaviors you were hoping to influence, or both. You don't have much, if any, formal authority over them and you cannot easily predict the specifics of the situation in which they might find themselves, so how do you get them to do what you want? Story is like mental software that you supply so your listener can run it again later using new input specific to the situation."

— Annette Simmons[10]

STORY MATRIX - CRAIG WORTMANN

Leadership Performance Skills

Story Types		Culture/Company	Execution	Sales	Service	Teamwork	Me
	Success	"Safety valve" Client delight Unexpected raise "I'm with you" "We are still here" Enemy at the gates	Client delight Scrabble story "Stay on target" How big is an acre? Dog bites child Beb's boom mic	Written any books? Thank you notes Adding value Gale's best day Lisa bringing kids books	Placido Domingo "Amazing" & "fun" Bag boy	Retreat '02 USB all-nighter Columbine A client becomes an investor	Van's birth Life is like a train Leaving big blue Dad's proud Dist. Achiever Forgiveness Jill - how am I doing?
	Failure	Tidal wave Circle time I KJC's story Audit CEO Perfect storm	Circle time II Oskaloosa trip Garfield's broken sidewalk Financial planning Seminars Rip Van Winkle Buttons to zippers to Velcro	Tidal wave USB all-nighter Trans vs. Rel Greatest skill?	Too many assumptions Win one for the team And then there were 7...	Columbia Shuttle Einstein's relativity	Losing control Not hired Everything's awesome? Drop Forge Playing the "greatest hits" Gyp line
	Fun	Story of wolf Van: send an e-mail Weirdest week "Sir, we have a major medical oppty" Hunter: talk to the hand	"Betty" & "Fred" Che-che...che-che...	Mom's watch Email to CEO FYMTGE Set your phasers to stun	Big hat "Betty"& "Fred" Name the ethics line	His best skill Boom	"I've got some ideas" Jungle stories Driving through Iowa with Dad Mom never giving up
	Legends	Nabisco air force Guru/master tea cup Trump $1.5BB Whisker from a tiger Stanford: foreign policy crisis	Apollo II Rock/sand/water Good enemy of great Gerstner - "tell me about" Crossing the chasm Henry Ford: "black"	Glengarry Martin Luther King Churchill Columbia shuttle Truth, naked and cold	Nordstrom's Southwest FedEx Traveler arriving at gates	US Hockey team Apollo II Gates and Dell FedEx Practice makes perfect	

FIGURE 5.2 Story Matrix: Entrepreneur

The boundaries between these different categories are not hard and fast. A story about how a project went well could just as soon be found in the "Execution" category as in the "Leadership" category. Many times, the same story can be found in multiple places on the Story Matrix because the telling of the story can focus on different elements, depending on what performance challenge is being addressed.

The one category on the Story Matrix that should be present on any type of leader's matrix is the category called "Me." The pur-

VAN'S BIRTHDAY

One of the Me stories that I tell is about the birth of my son, Van. When my wife was five weeks away from her due date, I was out of town on business in Bloomington, Indiana. Late one night, I got the call from my wife, Jill, that she was in labor and the doctor had told her to get to the hospital. Bloomington, Indiana, is 250 miles from Chicago, where we live. I was in the car within five minutes, driving 100 miles per hour, heading for Chicago—hoping to make it in time.

Jill made it to the hospital and I was in cell phone contact with her mom, who was giving me periodic updates as I got closer and closer to Chicago. My phone rang as I flew across the Chicago Skyway, about 45 minutes from home. Our son, Van, had arrived, happy and healthy. I had missed it. Arguably, the most important event in any person's life, and I had missed it. My son was 45 minutes old when I met him for the first time.

But, instead of feeling sorry for myself, I held the loudest, most joyous one-man party that the Chicago Skyway has ever seen! To this day, I look upon that experience like this: it only matters that Van and Jill were fine, not whether I was there. This story helps people understand how I look at the world. It's much more meaningful than just telling someone, "I tend to be a positive person."

pose of these Me stories—stories of personal success, failure, and fun—is to encourage leaders to let employees get to know who they are and what values they hold. Just as failure stories are important to a leader's ability to build strong connections with people, Me stories allow people to look inside you. Me stories share your values, what you truly care about, and what makes you tick.

USING YOUR STORY MATRIX

The last page of this book is *your* Story Matrix. As you recall your stories, capture them on this Story Matrix that reflects the areas you most need to influence. In order to put the Story Matrix into action, just "peel" back the top layer of the Story Matrix, and another layer is revealed, as in Figure 5.3. This layer is where the story gets outlined and applied to different types of challenges. In this layer, each story is annotated with three elements. First, the

"Personal stories let others see 'who' we are better than any other form of communication. Ultimately people trust your judgment and your words based on subjective evidence. Objective data doesn't go deep enough to engender trust."

— Annette Simmons[11]

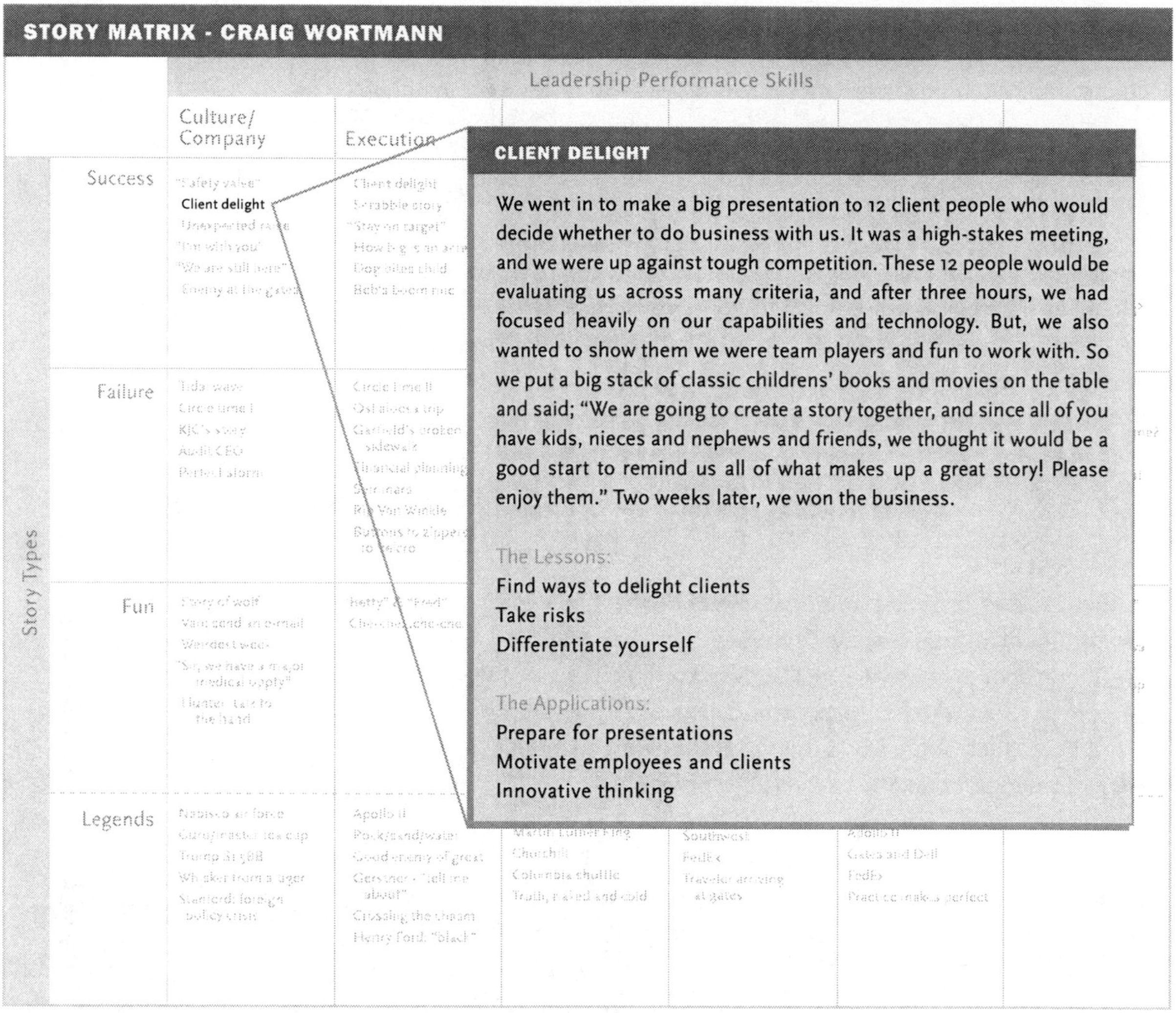

STORY MATRIX - CRAIG WORTMANN

		Leadership Performance Skills				
		Culture/ Company	Execution			
Success		"safety valve" Client delight Unexpected raise "I'm with you" "We are still here" Enemy at the gate	Client delight Parrable story "Stay on target" How big is an acre Dog bites child Bob's Lemon rind			
Failure		Tidal wave Circle time I KJC's story Audit CEO Parted storm	Circle time II Oshkosh's trip Garfield's broken sidewalk financial planning Star hero Rip Van Winkle Buttons to zipper to Velcro			
Fun		Story of wolf Van's send an e-mail Weirdest two-er "Sir, we have a major medical supply" Hunter, take to the hand	"Betty" & "Fred" Chevron one-on-one			
Legends		Teamsco or force Guru/master tea cup Trump 31,588 Whisker from a tiger Stanford foreign policy crisis	Apollo II Pork/sand/water Good enemy of great Gerstner - "tell me about" Crossing the chasm Henry Ford "black"	Martin Luther King Churchill Columbia shuttle Truth, naked and cold	Southwest FedEx Traveler arriving at gates	Apollo II Gates and Dell FedEx Practice makes perfect

CLIENT DELIGHT

We went in to make a big presentation to 12 client people who would decide whether to do business with us. It was a high-stakes meeting, and we were up against tough competition. These 12 people would be evaluating us across many criteria, and after three hours, we had focused heavily on our capabilities and technology. But, we also wanted to show them we were team players and fun to work with. So we put a big stack of classic childrens' books and movies on the table and said; "We are going to create a story together, and since all of you have kids, nieces and nephews and friends, we thought it would be a good start to remind us all of what makes up a great story! Please enjoy them." Two weeks later, we won the business.

The Lessons:
Find ways to delight clients
Take risks
Differentiate yourself

The Applications:
Prepare for presentations
Motivate employees and clients
Innovative thinking

FIGURE 5.3 Using the Story Matrix

story itself is outlined more fully so that we remember it. Second, the "moral" or "lessons" of the story are captured. Third, the "applications" are jotted down next to the moral of the story in order to provide the leader with a better understanding of what types of situations are best addressed with this particular story. Some people do this naturally, but the structure of the Story Matrix is designed to support those of us who need to be reminded of the lessons and applications of our stories.

Using the Story Matrix in Figure 5.3, a leader might, for instance, tell his team this story about client delight as a way to prepare them for an important presentation. The story illustrates how he wants them to think about ways to differentiate themselves in that presentation.

Figures 5.4 through 5.7 provide several examples of different types of Story Matrices for different types of leaders, including a senior executive, middle manager and sales leader, and even the Story Matrix of an entire division of a large enterprise.

STORY MATRIX – PARTNER/SENIOR EXECUTIVE

		Leadership Performance Skills					
		Motivation	Client Relationships	Teamwork	Engagement Scoping	Managing	Me
Story Types	Success	One down, two to go; And then it happened	Best in business Analysis failure/ relationship excellence	Friend or foe Friend or foe, part 2	Need a wide-angle lens! In and out of scope	Management can be fun! Santa's early this	Back in the day... Chosen path
	Failure	This is not fun. It's pouring No second guessing Poker face	The one that got away Hurts so bad Long fight				
	Fun	Hands in the middle You really do have g lives!	Genuine fun Tennis anyone? Late nights, bad pizza				
	Legends	Moon! Space race	The "Jerry Maguire" handshake				

FIGURE 5.4 Story Matrix: Partner/Senior Executive

ANALYSIS FAILURE / RELATIONSHIP EXCELLENCE

The project team worked for four months to deliver analysis that would drive major marketing decisions within a deadline. A quality review just before the deadline revealed data processing errors that rendered the recommendations useless with insufficient time to fix the analysis before the deadline. The team told the client and rather than being upset, they were overwhelmingly impressed by our diligence and honesty. Further, they chose to commit to the new marketing approach because we worked so effectively with them over the prior four months that they trusted our judgment and really understood what we were suggesting and why it would work.

The Lessons:
Clients admire integrity, even if it brings unpleasant news
Relationships develop by the way you work, not deliverables

The Applications:
People who are facing an ethical dilemma
People who are struggling to communicate a failure
People who are overcome with a fear of failure

STORY MATRIX – SALES LEADER

Leadership Performance Skills

Story Types		Planning	Execution	Follow-through	Presentations	Teamwork	Me
	Success	Looking out / Down the road / The 3 "P"s? / Whole lotta quote	See the future / Disaster averted / House of cards	Thank you note / The pen / Grab bag	Laws of defect / Full color / "Hello, Kitty?"	I'm buying... / Last man standing / Go home	Climbing the mountain
	Failure	That one gets I / Driver's permit	It happens / Spin Cycle / "Steve!" "No. I am Scott"	Ringing the bell / 26 urgent voice mails	Wearing plain and walking tall / Par five	Unprepared... / uncool	Always closing / Oversold / Intimidated
	Fun	Son of a preacher man? / Gravitational? / The 'closing' suit	False teeth / 24 hours in a row?? / Narcolepsy				
	Legends	World map	Not ready for prime time / Small but mighty				

FIGURE 5.5 Story Matrix: Sales Leader

"STEVE!" "NO. I AM SCOTT"

I was preparing for a very important client meeting where I would be meeting the decision-maker for the first time, after only seeing his picture in the Annual Report. I had done a lot of work getting a big proposal to this stage with his direct reports, and this would be the meeting where I would either close the deal or walk away empty-handed. I spent several hours preparing for any objections he might have and getting the documents ready. The appointed hour came. I stepped off the elevator in his office building just as the senior guy walked out of another elevator, so I looked at him and said: "Steve!" He said, very matter-of-factly: "Scott." I said: "No, my name is Jim." He frowned and said: "No, MY name is Scott!"

The Lessons:
The devil's in the details
If you make a mistake, admit it and recover

The Applications:
Cutting through the stress prior to a big presentation
Reminding people to cover the small details
Having some fun

STORY MATRIX – MIDDLE MANAGER, CONSUMER PACKAGED GOODS

		Leadership Performance Skills					
		Managing/ Coaching	Supply Chain	Teamwork	Planning	Recruiting	Me
	Success	"Gravitas" Surrounded… Umpires	Ethical dilemma Follow the leader "Can't get there from here…"	Angela	Mapquest? Love letter	Cold call Never stop talking	Farmer Don Happy Bottom
	Failure	No greater fan than me	Rotten berries bad day	Postage meter	Wrong turn "Uh, I faxed it yesterday"	Is this an interview? Seeking, searching, finding	Seen the worst? Same mistake, different day Swallowed whole
Story Types	Fun	Wildly unsuccessful? See a doctor	No no no	Swing batter	**Drop Forge** Pulp fiction	Good question! Good question Whoa, easy	Relief Good work, all started
	Legends	"If a tree falls in the forest…" "Do, or do not. There is no try."	Overnight Share less!				

FIGURE 5.6 Story Matrix: Middle Manager, Consumer Packaged Goods

DROP FORGE

I was asked to take over an important client, and I went to meet the senior guy for the first time. He ran a "Drop Forge" that made golf-club heads, which I figured was just another average manufacturing company. I was in for an unpleasant surprise! I showed up, dressed in suit and tie, starched and trying to look the part of a knowledgeable vendor. The senior guy came in wearing jeans, a greasy shirt and a frown. He obviously didn't suffer fools. We sat down at his grungy conference table, and I started to tell him about what we could do for him. About 90 seconds into my spiel, the drop forge, which turned out to be a 40-ton hammer dropping four stories and stamping out metal clubs, dropped and shook the whole room as if it were a serious earthquake. I jumped up and shouted "What was that?" The senior guy just stared at me as if I were completely stupid (very close to home, it turns out). He said, "The forge. We're a forge, or didn't you know that?" So, there I sat for the remainder of the meeting, every 90 seconds being all but thrown from my chair while I suffered through a horrible, lame explanation of what we might be able to do for this guy's company! I can still see this guy walking out and telling his staff about the hilarious look of terror I had when the forge dropped for the first time!

The Lessons:
Never meet a new client or partner without knowing about what they do
Don't forget the details like materials, dress code, etc. that can derail a meeting

The Applications:
Planning for a transition
Getting people prepared to face an unfamiliar situation
Having some fun

STORY MATRIX – A BUSINESS DIVISION

		Leadership Performance Skills				
		Culture/Company	Customer/Service	Execution	Productivity	Teamwork
Story Types	Success	Clash of Cultures Mutual? National Accounts Diversity	Concierge C Service Ramer be Se The Bear			
	Failure	Towel dispenser	Onion Ring			
	Fun	"Politician" joke	"Crotch Wate Idiot Card			
	Legends	Garden/Park/ Wilderness S O M	"Crotch Wate			

FIGURE 5.7 Story Matrix: A Business Division

CLASH OF CULTURES

Our organization was entertaining a merger with another large company. The merger looked great on paper and the economics made sense. So, inevitably, the two senior teams had to come together to discuss the sticky subject of how the leadership structure would work. One of our senior people is known for his collaborative style of management and thus his senior team was collegial and worked as a tight group that lacked hierarchical structure.

The other company, however, was run by the former governor of a large state, and his was a very hierarchical company. What the governor said was what got done, nothing more and nothing less. His was a command and control style and when the two teams got together, no one talked but the governor. He was to be called "Governor."

The two teams mixed like oil and water, and it didn't take long to establish that these two leadership teams would have a very hard time integrating into one entity. It took only one meeting to figure out that this merger was dead on arrival. The team walked away, and subsequently went on to merge successfully (and we continue to do so today) several times with more compatible teams and have created a large, successful enterprise.

The Lessons:

Culture is extremely important
We have a strong, positive culture
We have been very careful in selecting merger partners

The Applications:

Welcoming new people from our merger partners into the company
Helping new employees understand what leadership cares about
Having some fun
Communicating what's important to leadership and how culture is built

What does this process of matching a story to a performance challenge actually look like? Figure 5.8 shows how a leader (in this case, a sales leader) can target the right stories to impact specific skills that need development. Just as the story of client delight above helped the team think through their differentiators, the leader on the left-hand side of Figure 5.8 has a salesperson who needs to improve performance in three areas: follow-through, presentation skills, and closing. The leader uses his Story Matrix to select three stories that illustrate each of these performance issues. The stories he tells his salesperson provide context for the performance issues that she is facing, and are far more effective than just saying to her, "Hey Leslie, we need to work on a few things: improve follow-through, tune presentation skills, and work on closing."

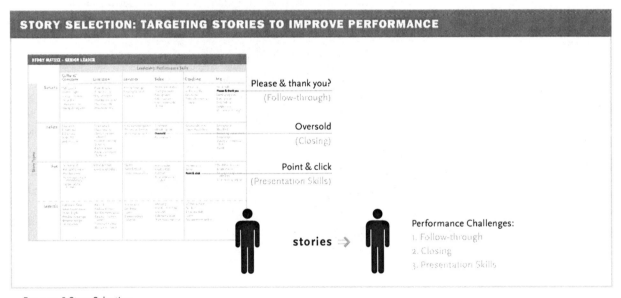

FIGURE 5.8 Story Selection

"As I see it, an effective leader, as he/she makes the rounds at his/her organization, must ask one...and only one... question: 'GOT ANY GOOD STORIES?'"

– Tom Peters[12]

Some stories you will find yourself telling over and over again, and that's okay. But also be sure to keep adding to your Story Matrix. Some clients have actually used the Story Matrix to look back "on the stories that we have been telling ourselves." In this way, the stories help explain why they have been performing the way they have. Similarly, these clients have often used the Story Matrix to create the future. They ask, "What stories will we be telling at the end of this year?"

The Story Matrix answers a fundamental question that we are probably not accustomed to asking: How do I get access to the best stories about this particular challenge I'm facing?

When we read books and hire consultants to help us tackle the tough challenges in our work and lives, we often ask the wrong question. We ask, "What should I be doing differently and better?" While this is a perfectly appropriate question, it's asked too early in the cycle of managing performance and leading people. How can we understand and take action on the *what* until we know the *whys* and *hows*? Those come from experiencing stories that illustrate the whys and hows of similar challenges. Only then do we truly understand the *what* so that we can take action.

This is a process. You need not have every cell of every category filled in. As long as you have one or two stories from your Win Book in each category, you will be prepared and well-served. As you fill in your Story Matrix, it quickly becomes a powerful tool that you can use to be more consistent and intentional in your communications. Now it is time to put that Story Matrix to use and tell your stories.

CHAPTER 5:
SUMMARY

THE BITS AND BULLETS

- The Story Matrix is a tool that provides a way to categorize and access our stories.

- The Story Matrix allows us to look at our library of stories and gives us context to think deliberately about how to use a particular story to impact performance.

- The vertical axis of the Story Matrix is made up of the different types of stories that all leaders should be telling.

- The horizontal axis changes to mirror the most common challenges you face.

- Don't forget the "fun" layer of stories. Make it your responsibility to bring some fun to work.

- The Story Matrix is the "filter" that holds the gold nuggets after the mud and grit have been shaken away.

THE PICTURES

Sample Story Matrix
While the vertical axis stays the same, the horizontal axis is customized depending on how you serve the organization and your people

Story Matrix: Entrepreneur
Because an entrepreneur oversees all aspects of a small organization, he or she will have broad categories of stories like "Leadership," "Service," and "Sales"

Using the Story Matrix
Behind each story on the matrix, there is a short vignette, the lessons, and the applications of the story

Story Matrix: Partner/ Senior Executive

Story Matrix: Sales Leader

Story Matrix: Middle Manager

Story Matrix: A Business Division

Story Selection
Depending on the performance challenge you are facing, apply the right stories that help illustrate how to tackle that challenge

THE STORIES

When Have You Failed?
Are you sharing failure stories? If not, you are missing a tremendous opportunity to help yourself and others

Van's Birthday
Me stories are the stories you tell about yourself that illuminate who you truly are and what you believe in

Chapter 5:
MY THOUGHTS AND IDEAS

6

CHAPTER 6:

THE STORY COACH

"Either you are going to tell stories that
spread, or you will become irrelevant."

– SETH GODIN[1]

TELLING STORIES

The Story Coach is the third tool in the toolbox. The technique of telling stories is a big subject. Many books have been written on how to tell stories. In this book, however, there is an assumption that because the stories that we have captured are (mostly) our own, telling them does not require specialized skills. It is far more important that we have captured the two key elements to a good story—the linkage to performance and our own honest voice—than whether we are fantastic storytellers.

Many people make the mistake of thinking that when it comes to telling a story, they need special skills that only a precious few have. This is false. We don't need to become performers with dramatic skills in order to captivate an audience. We already tell stories every day. There are just a few simple things to keep in mind when telling a story. We are not just doing it for the sake of telling stories (although that's a lot of fun); we are telling *our* stories that are *heading in a certain direction*.

What does a good coach always say? Play your position. Be yourself. Stay loose. Be open to possibilities as they unfold. Don't try to do too much. Think about what you could have done better.

It is the same with telling stories. *The right intentions combined with a truthful and engaging story create the spark that ignites performance.*

Telling the right stories at the right times is a lot like learning to be a good athlete. A good athlete develops habits of preparation, such as stretching and diet, and then aims at certain performance measures, whether those be time, distance, endurance, or points. Just as athletes do, we must develop habits that are consistent with the performance and results we desire.

Like the Win Book and Story Matrix, the Story Coach is designed to help you form these good habits that will keep you strong and healthy in the game. It is a set of criteria—or habits—that every leader should be practicing until it becomes second nature. The Story Coach uses the acronym "IGNITE" to provide you with a clear and easy way to remember the components of a great story.

IGNITE

The Story Coach is a simple technique to help people take action on the stories they have captured that will make a difference for them—and for everyone around them. Figure 6.1 outlines the Story Coach, and how the critical elements of telling a story combine to ignite performance. These elements are straightforward, and do not require dramatic skills. Using the Story Coach, your stories will be focused and natural, and they will make a connection with people.

"We don't think ourselves into a new way of acting, we act ourselves into a new way of thinking."

– LARRY BOSSIDY AND RAM CHARAN[2]

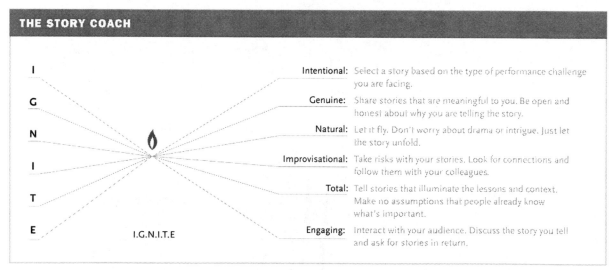

THE STORY COACH

I		
G		
N		
I		
T		
E	I.G.N.I.T.E	

Intentional: Select a story based on the type of performance challenge you are facing.

Genuine: Share stories that are meaningful to you. Be open and honest about why you are telling the story.

Natural: Let it fly. Don't worry about drama or intrigue. Just let the story unfold.

Improvisational: Take risks with your stories. Look for connections and follow them with your colleagues.

Total: Tell stories that illuminate the lessons and context. Make no assumptions that people already know what's important.

Engaging: Interact with your audience. Discuss the story you tell and ask for stories in return.

FIGURE 6.1 The Story Coach—IGNITE

I for Intentional

A good coach always says, "Play your position." Same as it is with telling stories.

You have captured many stories on your Story Matrix that apply to many different types of performance challenges. The first key of the Story Coach is to be intentional with your story. Select a story to tell with a certain lesson in mind. If you are facing an "execution" challenge, pick a story from that cell of your Story Matrix and think about the lessons—or moral—of the story.

Being intentional means that you have selected a story to tell that contains a lesson that you hope people derive from the story. But being intentional also means you don't leave that lesson or moral to chance. Once you have told your story, review your intentions with your audience to ensure that they "got it." One of the best ways to ensure that the moral of the story has been heard is to stay focused—play your position—and not stray or try to tackle more than one challenge at a time.

If your story meanders too much, or tries to weave together too many disparate themes, your audience will be lost. Better to focus in on one key lesson and drive it right into the heart of the problem.

Telling stories doesn't have to be mysterious, full of hidden meanings and subplots. When you are intentional and genuine, the stories are very straightforward. There is nothing wrong with saying to someone, "Here's what I was going for in that story. I wanted it to illustrate how we can tackle this challenge. I hope that you saw the decisions that those people made are similar to our own. Did you see that?" Our stories should not be treated like literature or movies where people have to discern the intent of the storyteller. You are standing right there; tell people your intentions! The story below, "The Legend of the Archer," demonstrates how to stick your story in the center of the target.[5]

"Do you have a storytelling plan? I believe this needs to become an essential part of any marketing plan or business plan—something that every nonprofit, start-up, big business and politician that intends to succeed must draft."
— SETH GODIN[3]

"Most leaders, in preparing for presentations, make sure that they have the right slides when they should focus instead on having the right stories."
— IAIN MACKENZIE[4]

THE LEGEND OF THE ARCHER

Once there was a maggid, or traveling teacher, who always told stories. It didn't matter if you came to him with a point of law that you wanted explained, a failing marriage that you wanted to discuss, or a grief that you wanted soothed. No matter what the problem, the maggid would tell a story.

One day a rabbi asked him, "There are sermons you could give, books you could read from, prophets who could be quoted, lectures you could deliver. Why do you always answer every question with a story?"

Of course, the maggid replied, "Let me tell you a story."

"There was once a general who decided to take up a hobby—archery. But being a general, he pursued his hobby like he would conquer a country. It was not enough to relax and enjoy himself. No, he had to be the best archer ever born. He read every book on the subject. He hired the finest teachers from all over the world. He bought the most expensive bow and arrows. Still, he could not hit the bull's eye every time, and it bothered him!

"One day he was riding in his coach to a military meeting when he saw the most amazing sight. He called for his driver to stop, jumped out of the coach, and ran into a nearby farmhouse, bursting in on the family eating dinner.

"'Where is he?' he demanded. 'Where is the master archer who did that?' He pointed out the window at their barn. On the side of the barn were many targets drawn, and in the center of each one was a single arrow.

"The family shrugged and pushed forward a little boy about ten years old. 'You! A mere lad is able to do what I cannot! Show me your secret.'

"The boy led the general out to the barn. He provided him with a crudely made bow and arrow and said, 'Do as I do.' He pulled back his bowstring, aimed in the general direction of the barn, closed his eyes, and let the arrow fly.

"Then he put down the bow, picked up a paint brush, dipped it into a bucket, and began to paint the target around the arrow."

The maggid stopped and looked at his colleague who was listening intently. "A good rabbi is a storyteller who knows so many tales that he can fit one to any situation."

G for Genuine

A good coach always says, "Be yourself." Same as it is with telling stories.

In your organization and in your life, people know you a certain way. They know your personality and your style. They have a sense for how you react to different situations and pressures. And, mostly, they know what to expect of you. Trying to tell stories to make you look smarter or more charismatic won't help ignite performance. It's not genuine; it's fake, and people can see right through to the real you. This is another reason that we must tell as many failure stories as we tell stories of successes. We've all seen leaders who tell nothing but success stories, and after a few of these, we know in our gut that this leader is not being genuine. He is trying to be someone he is not.

This is one of the reasons why the Story Matrix is focused on capturing your own stories, not abstract parables or myths. Although these story types can be very powerful and helpful (indeed, this is the function of the "legends" section of the Story Matrix), they can be overused and perceived as fake. The advice for you to be yourself is easy to follow if you are telling your own stories.

One of the advantages of telling your own stories is that you don't have to memorize them. You have lived them, and they are yours. As soon as you have to memorize something, your delivery shares the same stilted, point-by-point tedium of the average PowerPoint presentation. If a story doesn't feel right, don't tell it. It won't be genuine and authentic.

Does the story reflect something about you? That is, does the story help people understand what you value, how you make decisions, and how you look at your experiences? One of the main reasons people make a connection to you as a leader is through an understanding of what makes up your character. The only way this can happen is via your demonstration of these values through your actions and through the stories you tell.

N for Natural

A good coach always says, "Stay loose." Same as it is with telling stories.

Because stories are how we experience the world, they come naturally. And when we tell a story, we should not be afraid to be natural. Forget about the rules of business. If you get wrapped up in a story, chances are very good that those around you are wrapped

> "The first few tries of anything new are like the first few pancakes...you have to throw them out."
>
> — Russ Roberts[6]

> "In seeking truth, you have to get both sides of a story."
>
> — Walter Cronkite

> "The facts and data all around us soon disappear, but the stories continue to rattle around in our heads."
>
> — Marty Siegel[7]

up in it too. Let it fly. If it's got emotion, show it. If it makes you scared or nervous, admit it. No one can fault you for feeling the power of a story or reliving some of the emotions it evokes.

Annette Simmons, in her book, *The Story Factor*, puts it like this:

"There are two main reasons people hold back when they tell a story. The first reason is that they are afraid they will look stupid, corny, manipulative, or 'unprofessional.' Some people are afraid that telling a story is going to damage their credibility in some way. It is crazy, but at times we are afraid to be human in front of other human beings, especially when we want to impress those human beings. So we act 'professional' and keep things tidy, logical, and rational. We use arguments that make sense, can be proven empirically, and lead to a logical conclusion. Unfortunately our delivery becomes uptight, clinical, emotionless, and b-o-r-i-n-g."[8]

Toastmasters International, a great organization with a mission to "help men and women learn the arts of speaking, listening, and thinking," has compiled a list of tips for speaking to groups. Most of them encourage speakers to know their material, know the audience, and be comfortable with the surroundings. This is all great advice. But when you are telling stories at work to your colleagues and your clients, most of this comes naturally. After all, they are *your* stories, so getting comfortable with the material should be easy. And presumably, you are also very familiar with the people involved (or at least most of them) and the surroundings. These are big advantages that already tilt the playing field in your favor as you begin to use your stories.

Remember, if you are nervous telling a story—heck, even if you think you just butchered a story—chances are that you have inspired someone to tell their own story. Such is the nature of stories. We all have them. They are dying to get out into a work world that can be, at times, very sterile and boring. You are modeling the way for people. You are acting your way into a new way of thinking and showing people that they too can do it.

"Rather than abandoning stories, clinical researchers and policy makers must come to appreciate that stories are meaningful, must recognize representative stories when they hear them, and must learn to retell these stories well."

— JOHN STEINER[9]

THE HERO'S JOURNEY

Shortly after joining WisdomTools as its CEO, I called the top people in the company together and we ran through a very powerful exercise together. We spent two hours telling each other stories about how things could go wrong with this business. We invented stories about making critical mistakes. We made up stories about the company failing and having to let go of our employees. We talked about what the letter to our shareholders would say and what it would feel like. It was an intense, emotional experience for all of us.

After two hours, we turned the conversation to telling stories of the company's success. We told stories about how the company would not only survive, but thrive. We told stories of delighted clients and engaged employees. We talked about building a strong community around the company and what it would feel like to report this success to our shareholders and our people.

That day, we touched both ends of the emotional spectrum. Our conversation became a metaphor for our company's journey— the hero's journey. We knew there would be ups and downs and successes and failures. But because of that conversation, we were more prepared to deal with the inevitable hurdles and we were better able to build tools and processes that would enable us to actually realize the great stories.

I for Improvisational

A good coach always says, "Be open to possibilities as they unfold." Same as it is with telling stories.

> "Oral storytelling is an improvisational art form, in many ways akin to jazz."
> — WIKIPEDIA ENTRY FOR STORYTELLING[10]

At first glance, it would appear that being more "improvisational" contradicts the need to be more "intentional" with our stories. Not so. Remember, the purpose of the Story Matrix is to help organize stories into categories that can then be matched to specific performance challenges. Each story has one or two "insights"—key takeaways—that throw light on a problem.

By capturing your stories with your Story Matrix, you will *be more prepared to be improvisational.* In improv training, you are asked to get up on the stage "with nothing in your mind." This is the hardest and scariest technique to learn in improv because we are taught from our earliest years to always be prepared. Now we

"Remember, stories aren't stories until they are told."

— DAVID HOLT AND BILL MOONEY[11]

are being told to be present, empty your mind, and just to react to what's going on around us. We are all nervous when we get on a stage, whether at an improv show or in a business meeting. We are nervous because we care. It's what makes improv so fascinating. In order to succeed in improv, we have to literally take whatever is offered and use our nervousness to our advantage.

Being improvisational means taking risks. If you are not willing to take a risk, why should your people follow you? There is only one hard and fast rule in improv. It's called "yes, and."[12] "Yes, and" means that you take what you are given. If you get on the stage with another person and that person looks at you and says, "Boy, what a boring wedding," you can't say, "We aren't at a wedding, we are at the auto repair shop." It just doesn't work. You have to say, "*Yes, and* the groom looks like he's had a few too many!" This gets the scene rolling and now the two of you can construct something meaningful.

Used correctly, the "yes, and" rule has profound impact on performance in business too. Again, we have to take what we are given. We are better leaders if we don't constantly try to tell people that some situation is different than what they are actually experiencing. If the story of where we are heading isn't so grand, we can't say, "All is well, folks! We are on the right track. Don't worry! No, really, all is well!!"

We have to select our stories with care. And we have to be honest. We should be telling stories that say, in essence, "Yes, and this looks grim. We've certainly been in better shape. Let's talk about how this could look if it went the right way and see what we can learn from it." We have all followed leaders who gave us the rosy picture no matter what. And they had zero credibility. After the first couple of empty platitudes, we stopped listening and just tried to stay out of the way.

THE STORY OF THE WOLF

An eccentric client of mine once challenged me to make up a story in front of an audience of 100 of his employees. I was standing on a stage in a theatre-type auditorium and had just finished a talk about leadership and service. He unplugged my laptop from the projector, plugged in his own, and brought up a picture of a wolf howling at the moon. He then said, "Craig, tell us a story about this wolf!"

In a moment of clarity, I turned the challenge around on my audience. I said, "Better yet, let's do this together. What is this wolf doing?" The audience's response was truly incredible. Someone volunteered that this wolf was singing a song. Another said that he was calling out to his family in joy. Another said that he was telling anyone who would listen that he was happy to be alive. What quickly became clear is that this audience saw nothing but positives. They were all optimistic that this wolf was happy and was simply howling about it.

It was a powerful few minutes for me. Here, I had just given a speech about leadership and service. And this audience was now demonstrating—in real time—one of the keys to being a great leader and providing superior service: a positive, optimistic outlook. I pointed this out to them and they were stunned. I then turned to my client and said, "That's the story of the wolf. And it's also the story of why this group truly understands leadership and service."

T for Total

A good coach always says, "Don't try to do too much." Same as it is with telling stories.

Storytelling pros from Aristotle almost 2,500 years ago to Robert McKee in the present day have coached us to focus on one core truth of a story, and not to dilute the story. You peel back the top layer of the Story Matrix to reveal the lessons and applications of the story—the core truth. And when you tell that story, people will understand the core truth.

Being total with your stories means balancing the need to be thorough with the need to be concise. One of the by-products of being awash in information is that we tend to find shortcuts. Often, these shortcuts end up in bullet points, as we saw in the Humpty Dumpty figure in Chapter 3.

"Selecting the facts, sequencing them, and picking a place to begin and end always alters the meaning of the facts. Your story creates meaning and meaning is by nature subjective. History is merely a sequence of stories we tell ourselves that helps us build assumptions about cause and effect."

– ANNETTE SIMMONS[13]

"Although businesspeople are often suspicious of stories for the reasons you suggest, the fact is that statistics are used to tell lies and damn lies, while accounting reports are often BS in a ball gown—witness Enron and WorldCom."
— ROBERT McKEE[14]

"Storytelling is the creative demonstration of truth. A story is the living proof of an idea, the conversion of idea to action."
— ROBERT McKEE[15]

A story that is "total" unfolds both the lessons and the context relevant to the listener. In order to ensure that you are capturing the lessons and the context, focus on the core truth of the story—why the story addresses a particular challenge. The more you focus on this core truth, the more people will see the fit between the story and the challenge it is addressing.

But then also question the assumptions you are making. How did you come to understand the lessons of this story? What did you think the first time you heard it? Look for leaps that you've made that others may not understand. You can even use your story to highlight these assumptions, making them explicit.

If you have been total in telling your stories, then you have built for your people what Annette Simmons calls "mental software."[16] When you are not around and your people are facing a tough issue, this mental software helps people make good decisions, and good decisions translate into better performance. People may not remember every aspect of the story, but they remember what happened and why it happened that way, and this helps them as they face their own challenges.

Being total in telling your stories also means acknowledging that the stories don't always fit the situation perfectly. Sometimes people will challenge the story. They will question your own understanding of the story or your intentions in telling the story. This presents another opportunity to open up a dialogue and use the story to learn. You may find that you disagree about the core truth of the story. That is okay. A disagreement about the lessons is a great way to problem-solve. One thing is certain: even a story that has different messages for different people will still do a better job of improving performance than bits and bullets.

E for Engaging

A good coach always says, "What could we have done better?" Same as it is with telling stories.

What happens at the end of just about every game you can think of, whether it's professional football or Pee Wee Hockey? The teams shake hands. This teaches sportsmanship, and it's another one of those sports habits, like exercise, from which the business world can learn a lot. In a very real way, shaking hands is

"Stories, then, can be a means to discover something completely new about the world. The value of stories, however, is not just in their telling, but in their retelling. Stories pass on to newcomers what old-timers already know. Stories are thus central to learning and education."
— JOHN SEELY BROWN AND PAUL DUGUID[17]

another way of acknowledging that we are all in this together. Win or lose, we are trying our hardest and always learning.

Stories are engaging for all of the reasons we have explored. But the engagement doesn't stop with the end of the story. That is only the beginning. Our stories should engage people while we are sharing them, but they should also serve to open people up for reactions, thoughts, and additional ideas. When good coaches sit their teams down after a win or a loss, they ask what could have been done better. Similarly, we should be asking our listeners how the story could have ended differently. What do they take away from the story? What do they disagree with, or what don't they like about it? How can the story help them the next time they are facing this same challenge?

Unlike most communications within business, a story is two-way communication. A teller and a listener or listeners engage together in a story. And unlike most of the memos and e-mails we get and the conferences and training we attend, we can react and question in real time. This is where the gears of better performance start turning. We are not being tested; we are simply discussing what we've heard. As we engage in a discussion of the story, we are opening up the story to other perspectives.

As leaders, when we engage a group after we have told a story, trust gets built. We are demonstrating our trust of others by the very act of telling a story, and we are showing that we are open to possibility by asking for reactions from the group.

The Story Coach is meant to be a sort of checklist for telling stories. Like the list you make for your camping trip, these are the things that you absolutely have to bring because if you find yourself out in the wilderness without them, you may end up cold and wet.

USING THE STORY TOOLS: A SIX-STEP PROCESS

In this part of the book, we have explored three distinct tools: the Win Book, the Story Matrix, and the Story Coach. The Win Book is the tool you can use to capture your experiences and stories. The Story Matrix is the tool that provides ready access to your stories so that you can quickly apply them to performance challenges. The Story Coach helps you tell your stories in such a way as to maximize your impact. As with any set of tools, the key is finding the method that works best for you, not following a rigid standard.

> "If you always 'get straight to the point' there may be times when you wonder why you are the only one there."
> – Annette Simmons[18]

> "The teacher and the taught together create the teaching."
> – Eckhart Tolle[19]

> "The greatest value of a good cognitive metaphor—as it makes no pretense of offering any definitive answers—lies in the richness and rigor of the debate it engenders."
> – Tihamer von Ghyczy[20]

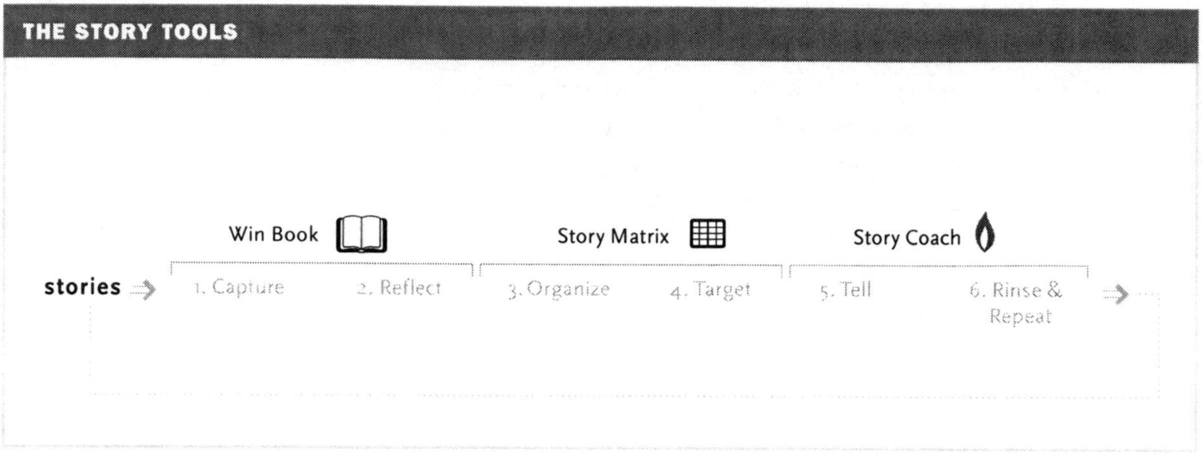

THE STORY TOOLS

FIGURE 6.2 The Story Tools

The six-step process for using these story tools is outlined below and illustrated in Figure 6.2:

1. **Capture.** Use whatever "filter" your have to capture your stories, whether it be a Win Book, a folder or notebook, your PDA, or the palm of your hand.

2. **Reflect.** Take a look through the "mud and grit" of your life and find the gold nuggets.

3. **Organize.** Write down those stories, anecdotes, and experiences in the most appropriate place on your Story Matrix (i.e., "This sounds like a leadership/success story.").

4. **Target.** The next time you are facing a challenge, take a look at your Story Matrix and think about what stories would be most effective for helping overcome that challenge.

5. **Tell.** Use the Story Coach to tell your stories, discuss the lessons, and ask for stories in return.

6. **Rinse and repeat!**

It's time to tell your stories. Just remember the tools and be yourself. Don't worry about whether you think you are a good storyteller. Don't worry about the distinction between "chef" and "cook." Just make food. No one will go away hungry.

CHAPTER 6:
SUMMARY

THE BITS AND BULLETS

- If you have the right intentions and are truthful in telling your stories, people will respond to you and they will be part of the solution.

- Applying and telling your stories to impact performance takes practice, like any other leadership skill.

- The Story Coach follows a simple acronym, IGNITE:
  - I—Intentional
  - G—Genuine
  - N—Natural
  - I—Improvisational
  - T—Total
  - E—Engaging

- Use the Story Coach to focus on the important elements of telling stories, and don't worry about whether or not you have dramatic skills. It's the sharing that gets results.

THE PICTURES

The Story Coach
IGNITE your performance and the performance of your people

The Story Tools
Putting the tools together to maximize your performance

THE STORIES

The Legend of the Archer
Don't just disperse information scattershot and hope for the best. Select a story that sticks right into the middle of the target

The Hero's Journey
Use stories to imagine the future, both good and bad, and then make the good stories come true

The Story of the Wolf
Don't be afraid to improvise, as long as you are genuine and honest

CHAPTER 6:
MY THOUGHTS AND IDEAS

PART FOUR

Let's put all of this together. We are aware of the problem that all leaders face, and we are armed with a solution and the tools to make it a reality. Now we need practice. In the following chapters, we will practice telling stories in different leadership situations with different challenges.

There are three critical skills leaders must demonstrate in order to be truly successful. The first is leadership. Leadership is living the behaviors and actions that you are expecting of others. It is creating an environment where people feel safe to take risks, make mistakes, and attempt to be great. In Chapter 7, we will meet a leader who is facing some very difficult challenges that require a solution that goes beyond pouring more information on the flames.

The second critical skill is selling. All leaders must be able to sell their decisions, perspectives, and modes of behavior. Chapter 8 shows us a leader who can sell. She is not infallible, but she does have a refined sense of when a story is necessary for pushing through results.

The third critical skill is motivating and inspiring people to be their best. A leader can't control the actions of others. All a leader can do is create the right context within which to perform and offer stories, guidance, and tools. Chapter 9 introduces a leader whose situation is very common. His challenge is to motivate people who are busy, overworked, and fragmented. Sound familiar?

These three skills are best implemented by telling stories, as they are very hard to effect any other way. In the last part of this book, let us practice and see these critical skills in action.

7

CHAPTER 7:

LEADERSHIP STORIES

"The choice for managers in organizations is not so much whether to be involved in storytelling—they can hardly do otherwise—but rather whether to use storytelling (a) unwittingly and clumsily or (b) intelligently and skillfully."
— STEPHEN DENNING[1]

CUTTING THROUGH THE NOISE

One part of the Hippocratic oath, the oath that is traditionally taken by physicians as they move out of schooling and into treating patients, is "First, do no harm." When individual contributors move into leadership positions, we should take the same oath. We should solemnly swear to "do no harm," which in our context means to help our people cut through the noise, not add more noise to the channel.

This is not a trivial task. Leaders are fighting momentum, deadlines, and sometimes themselves in trying to reduce the noise level in their organizations. It's the same challenge that parents have. Research shows that due to ubiquitous and nearly constant media exposure, our kids receive about 10,000 messages a year about eating: what to eat, how to eat, when to eat.

Let's just suspend disbelief for a moment and say that you have breakfast, lunch, and dinner with your kids every single day of the year, and in so doing, you can lead by example and show them how to make good decisions regarding what they eat and how to avoid all of the junk that's thrown at them. This means that, over the course of one year, you have about 1,000 opportunities to influence your kids' behavior when it comes to eating healthy foods. You are still overwhelmed by their media exposure by a factor of ten to one! How do you fight that?

I see only two ways of fighting that strong influence. One, you could unplug the TV, throw away the Game Boys, grab some vegetables, and move to the North Pole! Or, you can tell your kids stories about healthy eating that will contradict the messages they see (and, of course, you must demonstrate these stories as well). As with any tool, stories are not a silver bullet, but these stories will stick with them and influence the decisions they make. Is this easy? Certainly not. But it's better than the alternative.

Leaders in organizations have the same challenge. People are awash in information and messages. How do you cut through with the right message that people really need to follow? Not by adding more noise to the channel. You do it by telling them a story and engaging them to work out what to make of the lessons of the story.

OPEN SOURCE, NOT PROPRIETARY

"Story often simultaneously demonstrates values as it demonstrates skills."
— ANNETTE SIMMONS[2]

Sometimes, leaders behave more as "information brokers" than true leaders. This is dangerous and counterproductive. When leaders see themselves as information brokers, they tend to behave in a way that puts them in a power position, so that they are doling out information on an "as needed" basis. It's as if the most important information needed to run the business is proprietary to them, and flows from the top down. This creates, among other things, an environment where people tend to operate only in their narrow specialties and innovation is stifled. It can also create resentment for the leaders because people don't feel like their voices are ever heard.

> **DEFINITION: Open source,** *noun:* **1.** A philosophy of software development that harnesses the collaborative effort of otherwise unrelated developers to create and innovate new tools. **2.** Turns the proprietary, hierarchical development model on its head, by treating all developers as equals with important and innovative ideas to contribute. For an example of the open-source approach, look no further than the insanely successful Linux.

Instead, by being a leader who both tells, and calls for, stories, leaders create more of an open-source approach. Like open-source software development where every individual has the right to bring their best stuff to the project and fix anyone else's work, a leader who shares stories and asks for them in return builds an environment where innovation can spring from anywhere. People often feel more respect, which has all sorts of positive outcomes, such as employees taking responsibility for offering solutions versus waiting for answers, finding their passion, and simply being more engaged in the work.

Creating an open-source atmosphere also benefits leaders who need to share a lot of information. It creates a different dynamic in our presentations. Instead of only firing bits and bullets at people, we are swapping stories that relate to the bits and bullets. Leaders can rely on their people to fill in the gaps, and they don't have to hold all of the information. (It is impossible to hold all of the information anyway, so why act like we can?) In the average point-and-click presentation, people's minds are not engaging in telling stories and problem solving, but, instead, only reading slides (or just trying to stay awake!).

Finally, by creating an open-source atmosphere of sharing stories, the stories are constantly refreshed. Leaders should be asking, "How has this story changed? Are we operating under old assumptions?" In this way, people get a chance to share how new facts and insights may be changing the story, and what to do about it.

PUTTING IT ALL TOGETHER

We have a great opportunity to be a positive influence on the lives of those around us. By cutting through the noise and sharing stories, we can truly help people make better decisions and perform at a higher level. This opportunity exists every day, as we move from meeting to meeting and venue to venue. Sharing stories doesn't have to be dramatic. Don't wait for the perfect moment to tell your story; almost all moments are perfect. If we are doing our jobs well, we are weaving our stories into real situations and challenges faced by real people.

The Win Book, Story Matrix, and Story Coach tools provide the stories. You provide the delivery. Let's meet Brian and "listen in" on a day in the life of a leader like you.

> "Stories of identity convey values, build esprit de corps, create role models, and reveal how things work around here. More important than memos, mission statements, newsletters, speeches, and policy manuals almost ever are, stories, says Gardner, 'constitute the single most powerful weapon in the leader's literary arsenal.'"
>
> – THOMAS STEWART[3]

> "Nothing serves a leader better than a knack for narrative. Stories anoint role models, impart values, and show how to execute indescribably complex tasks."
>
> – THOMAS STEWART[4]

A LEADERSHIP STORY: "THE NEW NEWS BLUES"

The door of the cab swung open, and Brian threw some bills to the driver. "Thanks much," he said, looking at an attractive woman waiting to get in. "All yours!" he said as he launched himself toward his building at a dead sprint. Two minutes later and already out of breath, Brian burst into a conference room in the offices of his employer, DG Inc., and the apologies began.

"Folks, I am so, so sorry. I got stuck on the bridge. The cabbie couldn't do anything. We were stuck. There was a terrible storm! Golf-ball sized hail from out of nowhere! A dog ate my briefcase!"

A few annoyed chuckles rippled through the group as Julie, one of Brian's directors, turned to him. "Uh, okay, no biggie. But *you* called this meeting via urgent e-mail, at 8 PM last night, remember?"

"I know. I know. Look guys, I'm really sorry. I *did* get caught in traffic behind an accident. And I asked you guys to show up early. My apologies. Let me just chug some coffee and let's get into it." Brian, an executive at DG leading several teams of people and multiple projects, took off his coat and poured black coffee into a large cup as his colleagues shuffled some papers around. "Okay, as I mentioned last night, we got some bad news on the first customer survey of the year. Not good. The customers seem to like the *idea*, but not the way we are *executing* it. And I got one of those not-so-nice phone calls from upstairs—something about how we need to 'figure it out' and 'pull a report together *today*.' Very illuminating."

Kathy, another of Brian's reports, looked completely stressed out already. "Oh, great. More heat. More pressure. Just what we need. Another 'do-more-with-less' message from the top."

"Okay, everybody stay calm," said Brian. "We just need to put our heads together and figure out what to do."

Looking around the room, Julie said, "The first thing we need to do is to determine what, exactly, the customers are saying about the service."

Brian plugged the overhead projector into his laptop. "Bingo. You read my mind. I stayed up late last night pulling that together into a slide deck. The survey company we hired gave me all of the raw data and I cooked it, sort of. Can someone turn off the lights?"

Leaning over, Jose, a team leader, whispered to a colleague sitting next to him, "Good night, my friend. See you in the morning."

Brian opened his PowerPoint slides. "I started to pull together a report for the folks upstairs. We just need to lay out all the

pieces of the puzzle and then make a recommendation." Flipping
to the first slide and then clicking through several more showing
the data collection process and sample sizes, he said, "Here is a
quick review of the survey questions. You guys wrote them, so they
should be familiar. The good news is that the survey vendor thinks
we asked the right questions. The bad news is...well, the responses.
Any questions?"

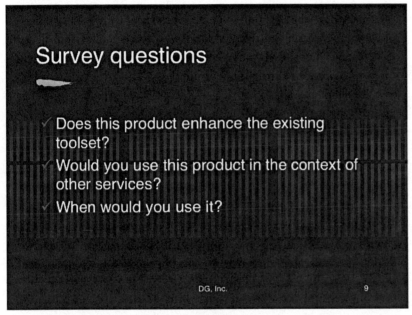

FIGURE 7.1 Slide from Brian's PowerPoint Presentation

"People actually do this statistics stuff for a living?" said Jose.
"I feel so sad for them."

"Come on guys, stay with me here. Seriously, any questions?"
He paused to look around the room. "No? Okay, let's look at some
of the sample responses. As you all well know, VM has announced
an offering that competes directly with ours, and getting some bad
vibes from our market right off the bat is a really bad sign. This
fight could be over before we get to the second round."

Julie broke in. "Let's narrow the responses into several groups,
so we know what we are dealing with."

"As usual, you are two steps ahead of me." The group then spent
a few minutes deciding what needed to be in the report and split up
the work. They agreed to regroup at noon in the same room.

A few minutes later, Brian rushed into his 9 AM meeting with the other senior leaders, once again late. Susan, the head of human resources, was just starting to click through a PowerPoint presentation on the new ethics guidelines that the company had put in place. "We need your support on this. As you can see from this slide, we have followed a very thorough and detailed process to get to this point. We have hired one of the best firms out there to help us carry the message out to the organization. Legal has formulated the ethics guidelines—thanks, Jim—and we are very concerned that if people don't understand and follow them, we will be open to significant risk. That's where you come in. We have prepared this presentation for you to give at your team meetings or off-sites. In addition, Jim and his team have an electronic version of the actual policy, and that will be sent to all employees, along with a signature page to be printed and signed by you and each of your employees."

Given his rough start to the day, Brian was harried, but trying his best to be supportive. "Susan and Jim, I really appreciate all the work you folks have done on this. I just wonder how I'm supposed to fit this in with the 50 other things that my people need to know? No offense, but will our people actually read this stuff?"

"I hear you," said Susan. "I know this is a lot to ask. But it's not optional. They *have* to read it, Brian. If they don't, we open ourselves up to all sorts of bad things."

"But isn't the true objective for them to be able to *act* on it? I mean, does just reading an ethics policy and signing something really protect us? Does the..."

"Yes, it does. In a way," said Jim, interrupting. "Look, if someone still does something stupid we are in for a big headache. But legally, we're better protected."

"I understand that. You all have convinced me how important this really is. But it just seems like a waste to do all this work for someone to just sign something. I can see this being received the same way people reacted to all of that other compliance stuff we went through last year. That was ugly."

"That's where the vendor we've hired comes in," said Susan, as she pulled up another slide. "They have prepared this slide presentation for all leaders, along with some recommendations for how to answer questions that will inevitably come up."

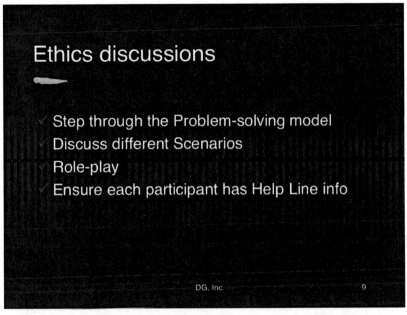

Figure 7.2 Slide from Susan's PowerPoint Presentation

When the meeting ended, Brian ran across the street for another cup of coffee. As he reflected on the meeting, he got increasingly frustrated by the amount of stuff on his plate and how most of it got only surface attention. Mumbling to himself, he said, "If we treat ethics, of all things, like just another 'sign-off' initiative, we're idiots."

"Sorry?" asked the cashier, looking strangely at Brian as he handed over a few bills.

"Huh? Oh, no, nothing. Just talking to myself again. Sorry."

Even though the café was playing the Rolling Stones' "Satisfaction" for the umpteenth time that week, Brian sat down at a table anyway and took a few minutes and to flip through his Win Book and Story Matrix, looking for a story that would shed some light on this ethics challenge. Twenty minutes later, he walked back into his office building. Kathy jumped into the elevator just as the door was closing.

"More coffee? You've got to cut back, man."

"No doubt," said Brian. "The sad truth is that I'm just getting started."

"How did the leadership team meeting go?"

"Truthfully? Frustrating. You've heard about the new ethics guidelines that are coming out?"

"Yeah. Big deal," Kathy said, shaking her head. "Those things are just a blip on the radar."

"Right! *That's* what's so frustrating! They shouldn't be! Think for a second how important that is."

"What's the big deal, Brian? I'm ethical. I'm not going to break any laws. Neither is the rest of your team."

"Kath, that's not the point. I know you are ethical. But think for a second how big this organization is. We do need people to make the right kinds of decisions. We need people who know how to manage their way out of difficult situations, or the company could really get into trouble. Haven't you read a newspaper for the past five years??"

"This is true," she said as she stepped off the elevator. "It *has* been one scandal after another. But Brian, do you actually think you are going to get people to pay attention long enough to learn something about this? Dream on, pal."

"Actually, I think I can," he said, thinking about a story he had seen on his Story Matrix. "And it has nothing to do with reading and signing paperwork. Do you know that we *have* had some problems?"

"Ethics violations? No."

"Well, we have," he said, leaving out the details. "A couple of years ago, one of our folks was working closely with a senior client executive who happened to be on the board of one of the city's sports teams. Because he was a huge sports fan, this client thought nothing of taking our guy to a bunch of games. Within reason, of course, there's nothing wrong with that. Unfortunately, the story doesn't end there. After a year of working with us, the client asked us to bid on a huge project. We won the bid, and everybody celebrated, *until* we discovered that the client had given our guy season tickets in return for a deep, deep discount."

Kathy was amazed. "Are you *kidding*? No way!"

"Wish I were."

"So what happened?"

"What do you think happened? That guy was quietly let go. And lest you think that it ends there, it doesn't. That guy is still looking for a job. And he has a young family. It's a tragedy, no matter which way you cut it."

Kathy paused to reflect on that. "That is a tragedy. I wonder why someone would do that? It makes no sense."

Jumping on her question, Brian said, "See, that's exactly the issue! It seems so obvious to you and me. But remember, this guy was just going along, doing his job like everyone else. I'm not excusing his behavior; not at all. It's just that it probably looked like just a couple of small favors to someone who was too close to the situation. The client was his friend. He needed to win the deal. What's the problem? That's why we need to take this stuff seriously. Don't get me wrong; the guy should be punished. No doubt. But we have to help people learn how to work their way out of these situations. We can't just continue to hope for the best."

"Well, for what it's worth, I think you just found the way to get people to listen." Kathy winked at Brian before starting to walk away down the hall. "Gotta go. I owe that crazy boss of mine a bunch of data by noon."

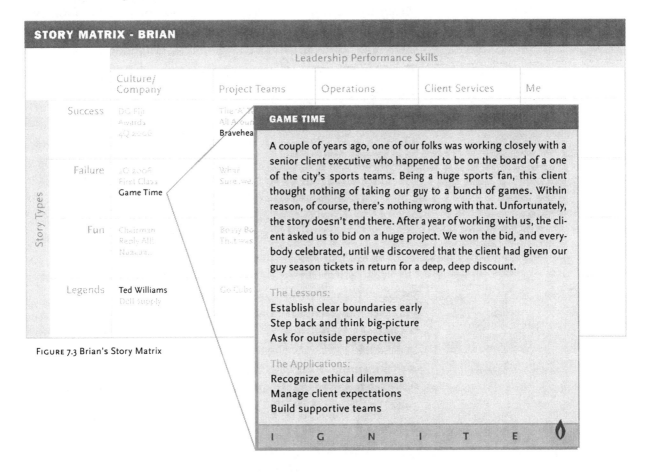

FIGURE 7.3 Brian's Story Matrix

STORY MATRIX - BRIAN

Leadership Performance Skills

GAME TIME

A couple of years ago, one of our folks was working closely with a senior client executive who happened to be on the board of a one of the city's sports teams. Being a huge sports fan, this client thought nothing of taking our guy to a bunch of games. Within reason, of course, there's nothing wrong with that. Unfortunately, the story doesn't end there. After a year of working with us, the client asked us to bid on a huge project. We won the bid, and everybody celebrated, until we discovered that the client had given our guy season tickets in return for a deep, deep discount.

The Lessons:
Establish clear boundaries early
Step back and think big-picture
Ask for outside perspective

The Applications:
Recognize ethical dilemmas
Manage client expectations
Build supportive teams

I   G   N   I   T   E

A couple of hours later, Brian walked into the noon meeting, on time and ready to go. Jose, snickering as usual, said, "What, no 'dog ate my paper' this time? I'm disappointed."

"Wise guy. Nope, ready for action this time. Talk to me, guys. Whatcha got, Jose?"

Jose handed Brian a bullet-pointed list of key points. "Here's a list of what we captured. I know it's not pretty, but it's a start."

"Yeah, it turns out that there is some really rich data in here," Julie chimed in. "It seems that the customers are trying to tell us something we haven't considered. Jose, tell Brian and the group about that one series of responses."

Jose spent a few minutes colorfully illustrating some findings that the original product development team didn't anticipate. Finishing his analysis, he said, "So, honestly, I'm not sure what to make of this, but it is definitely unexpected."

Brian was listening very closely, and obviously fascinated. "Jose, that was an excellent review. I don't really know yet what it means either, but I do know that there's something here that's important. Let's brainstorm on this for a few minutes. We should start..." Brian was interrupted by Danny coming in late. "Danny, thanks for coming. Before we brainstorm, Danny, what do you have for us?"

Danny was obviously caught off guard. "You know, I got pulled into another meeting this morning. I scratched out a couple of thoughts, but not much. I'll just listen in and then share my thoughts as we go."

"Danny, what meeting?" asked Brian with considerable annoyance in his voice. He was thinking about the report that he owed his boss at the end of the day.

"Just a thing I had to do. We had a problem with one of the reporting systems and I needed to jump on it."

Brian let it go for the time being. "Alright, well, let's brainstorm what we've got and see where it takes us. Julie, you go first."

The team spent the next hour generating ideas for how to craft a solution that will address the customers' issues and needs. Brian got excited as they wrapped up the meeting. "I'm stunned. Guys, this is exciting. We are finding out in real time how to beat VM. We have been reminded yet again that there is nothing like the voice of the customer to clarify things. But what we've discovered is out of the ordinary, and could take us to a much deeper, more profitable relationship with these customers! Okay, let's break again. You guys know what to do. Stay with me here. Bring your sections to my office at 4 PM and I'll stitch it together. Thanks much."

Looks were exchanged as Brian asked Danny to stick around for a few minutes after the meeting.

"I know this has already been a tough day."

"Look man, I'm sorry," said Danny, trying to avoid a confrontation. "I just got caught up."

"Danny, I specifically asked everyone to make this their number one priority. Was this distraction you had really an emergency?"

Danny was nervous. "No, I guess not. It did seem like you had everything under control when we walked out of our morning session, though."

"I disagree. Look, I was late to that meeting this morning, and I apologize. We are really under the gun. Everyone's watching us on this one. And you signed up to be on this team, knowing full well what the stakes were. You are a star on this team, but you've been fading in the late innings instead of coming on strong. What's the matter?"

"Nothing! I just got distracted. I've got a lot on my plate too, you know."

"You do. I know that. I really do. I just need you. This team is in danger without you contributing everything you've got." Brian thought about some notes he wrote in his Win Book after the last time one of his people dropped the ball. "This may sound crazy, but have you seen the movie *Braveheart*?"

"Of course," said Danny. "Who hasn't?" Imitating Mel Gibson's character, William Wallace, in a Scottish accent, he shouted, "WHAT WILL YOU DO WITHOUT FREEDOM?"

Brian started laughing. "Well, remember that scene? Remember what happened right after he said that?"

"Yup. It was a bloodbath. They fought the British and won."

"That's right. Think about it. They were outnumbered. They had no horses. Fewer weapons. Less training. And they were scared. But when William Wallace and his crew ran into battle, they were all swinging their swords as fast as they could. It was fight and win—or die. They were all clustered together, just swinging away and fighting. Wallace never had to look over his shoulder to see if his comrades were swinging. He knew they were swinging. He knew they had his back and they knew he had theirs. If he had stopped to look over his shoulder and make sure his guys were fighting, he would have been killed instantly."

"I hear ya," said Danny. "I do remember that scene—gory, but awesome. And I understand what you are saying."

"Danny, I'm not comparing myself to William Wallace; not at all. I'm just saying we have got to stick together. We can do this, and we can win. I know it. But you are one of the keys to winning."

"I'm with you," Danny said sincerely. "I am. Sorry I dropped the ball. Won't happen again."

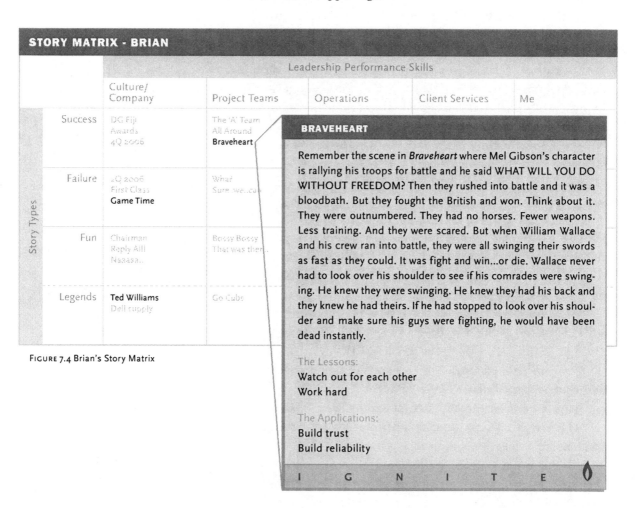

FIGURE 7.4 Brian's Story Matrix

A few minutes later, just as Brian sat down with Julie to build the report, Kathy walked into his office looking upset.

Looking up, he said, "Uh-oh. You look like you've seen a ghost. What's up?"

"Well," Kathy said sarcastically, "I should know better than to answer my phone. I just got off the phone with Steve at RW. It seems that our Denver office gave him some bad information, he acted on it, and it blew up in his face. Cost them a bunch of money and time. He's, how you say, *displeased?*"

Brian and Julie, at the very same time, said, "Please, no."

"Yup. He's not a happy camper; not at all. The phone call was a bumpy ride, to say the least. This side of my head started to melt off," she said, rubbing her left ear.

Julie was always thinking quickly. "So, we've got damage control to do."

"Yup."

"Is it bad to have 15 cups of coffee in one day?" Brian asked, massaging his temples. "Seriously, Kath, do I need to call him immediately?"

"No, I talked him down from the ledge. He's going to be okay. I just need to do something. I don't know what yet, but something. He's such a great guy and such a good customer, that I just feel like we need to go above and beyond for him. You know, just a 'we blew it but you know we are still here for you' message."

"What about a letter of apology from Brian, or even Laura?" offered Julie.

"No. That won't do it. He's resilient, so he'll be fine in a couple of days. We just need to make him feel like we learned from it and that we will double-check things from now on."

"What about just making that clear to him?" Julie said.

"I did. Sorry I keep shrugging you off Julie, I guess I'm just looking for something different. Something out of the ordinary."

Brian suddenly came alive. "Ah! You just reminded me of something we did a few years ago with our ZX client! I was working out of the Chicago office on that giant project with ZX. It was our first, so we were all completely stressed, knowing that this client was about 10,000 times more demanding than average. We were a couple of weeks into the project, and everything was going smoothly. But that was the problem."

"What? What do you mean?" Kathy asked, confused. "You've had too much caffeine."

"No, stay with me. Even in my caffeine-induced stupor, I can still make a point! The problem was, it was going too smoothly. We were everything they expected. No more. No less. We weren't making a great impression; we weren't making any impression. We couldn't find a way to really shine, such that we would rise above all of their other partners."

Kathy said hesitantly, "Okay, I'm starting to track you. Go on."

"We were just doing our stuff, and they were fine with it. But we were just bumping along the horizon, nothing too exciting. One day, a bunch of their very senior people came in to present a key component to the solution. It turned out that this component was very complex and it significantly changed what we needed to do. The senior client people called this component the "birthday cake," because it had a bunch of different layers and different features. They showed us a picture of the "birthday cake," and I swear it was the ugliest slide I've ever seen. They insisted that we change our approach to accommodate this new information, and they wanted to see our plan the next day. Needless to say, we were horrified."

Julie shook her head in recognition. "Oh, I heard about this. This happened right before I came to work here."

Brian continued. "It was great. We wrapped up that day and immediately got back together to figure out how to respond. We pulled in talent from all over the company. Thank goodness for technology. By 10 PM that night, we had our approach reconfigured. We were confident and ready. And that's when the real genius struck. Jennifer, the project leader, looked at us and said, 'We need a birthday cake.' We, of course, thought she had lost her mind. When we questioned her remaining thread of sanity, she said, 'Guys, they are going to like this approach. They really are. But you've been saying that we haven't been able to really wow them, right? So we are going to bring a big, huge birthday cake with multiple layers to the meeting tomorrow. That will get their attention!' Now we were sure that she had gone completely insane."

Kathy was locked on to the story Brian was telling. "What happened?"

Brian was laughing. "Well, Jennifer convinced us to find a bakery that was open at 7 AM the next morning and buy the biggest, most obnoxious birthday cake we could find. We snuck it into the conference room where we were meeting that day. As we wrapped up our presentation, the senior leaders were digging our approach, and they seemed genuinely pleased with our efforts. After they had confirmed that we were on target, Jennifer whips out the cake, candles and all, and says, 'Well, in that case, let's celebrate!' The place went nuts! The client was stunned, and everyone started laughing and joking at once. It was great. Even the stodgy senior folks were eating cake like they were kids at a birthday party."

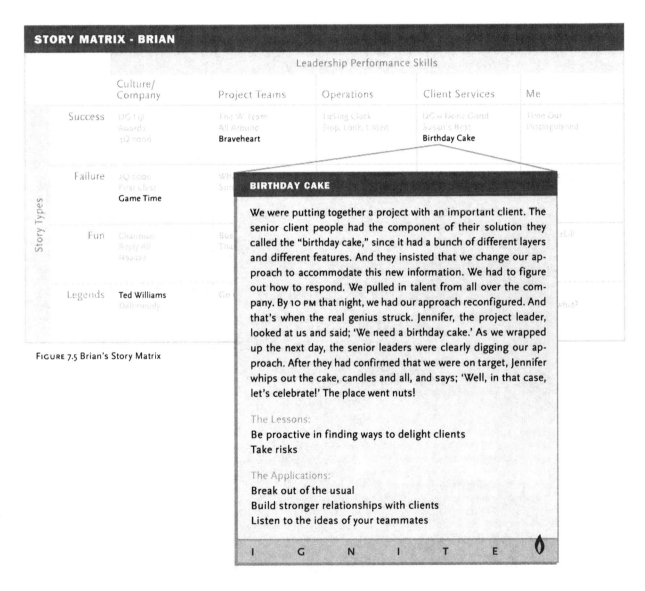

FIGURE 7.5 Brian's Story Matrix

STORY MATRIX - BRIAN

Leadership Performance Skills

BIRTHDAY CAKE

We were putting together a project with an important client. The senior client people had the component of their solution they called the "birthday cake," since it had a bunch of different layers and different features. And they insisted that we change our approach to accommodate this new information. We had to figure out how to respond. We pulled in talent from all over the company. By 10 PM that night, we had our approach reconfigured. And that's when the real genius struck. Jennifer, the project leader, looked at us and said; 'We need a birthday cake.' As we wrapped up the next day, the senior leaders were clearly digging our approach. After they had confirmed that we were on target, Jennifer whips out the cake, candles and all, and says; 'Well, in that case, let's celebrate!' The place went nuts!

The Lessons:
Be proactive in finding ways to delight clients
Take risks

The Applications:
Break out of the usual
Build stronger relationships with clients
Listen to the ideas of your teammates

I G N I T E

"That's great!" said Kathy. "What a great idea."

Brian was shaking his head. "It's crazy. I mean, on its face, it was a crazy idea. It was silly, and it had nothing to do with the actual work. But it set us apart. Just that little gesture set us apart from the rest of their partners. For months after that, we would walk into meetings with new client people and they would say, 'Ah, you're the birthday cake people!' or 'These are the *fun* people.' It made all the difference."

Kathy was now very fired up. "You know what? That's it; something like that. We just need to do something crazy for Steve that shows that we are human, but that we still care about him. Alright, the wheels are turning now. Thanks so much."

Later that same afternoon, Brian took the finished report up to the executive floor and delivered it to his boss, Laura.

Laura was obviously stressed about the customer feedback they were getting. "Brian, thanks for this. This new information is really getting me down. It was totally unexpected."

"I know. I'm disappointed too. But we've been here before, Laura."

Laura was not comforted. "Not with our biggest competition breathing down our necks. If this new service fails, Brian, we are open to being acquired. Then the game of musical chairs begins. You know what I'm talking about?"

"I look at it like this," said Brian, trying another approach. "We did a bunch of good research. We designed the offering based on that research. We rolled it out. And now we are finding out that some of the trade-offs we made in development were right on, and some weren't. Laura, it's like what the dean of Harvard Medical School once told the new students on their first day in med school. He said something like, 'We are going to teach you a lot. You are going to learn the accumulated wisdom of thousands of years of study of the human body. But remember, half of what we will teach you here is wrong—and the trouble is that we don't know which half.'

Laura turned more thoughtful. "Hmmm. Interesting. You know, that's true. That's what makes this business so hard. We never know until we know."

STORY MATRIX - BRIAN

		Leadership Performance Skills				
		Culture/ Company	Project Teams	Operations	Client Services	Me
Story Types	Success	DG Fiji Awards 4Q good	The 'A' Team All Around **Braveheart**	Ticking Clock Stop, Look, Listen	DG = Done Good Susan's Best **Birthday Cake**	Time Our Distinguished
	Failure	2Q good First Class **Game Time**	Wha? Sure we...can	Downtime	Follow-THREW ball? What ball?	Last pick F.I.L.D
	Fun	Chairman Ready All Naaaa...	Bossy Bossy That was then..	Midnight Call me Surely	Pizza breakfast Pimples	Hot b-rst sUN Boom
	Legends	**Ted Williams** Dell supply	Go Cubs	September again **Harvard Med School**	Look out!	Swedes You did what?

FIGURE 7.6 Brian's Story Matrix

HARVARD MED SCHOOL

It's like what the Dean of Harvard Medical School once told the new students on their first day in med school. He said something like, 'We are going to teach you a lot. You are going to learn the accumulated wisdom of thousands of years of study of the human body. But remember, half of what we will teach you here is wrong...and the trouble is that we don't know which half.'

The Lessons:
We are working with uncertainty
Demonstrate humility

The Applications:
Build business acumen
Manage without perfect information

I G N I T E

"Right. But, we can continue to anticipate. And there's a silver lining. I think you are going to find something unexpected in this report. I'm looking forward to hearing your thoughts because I believe that we have found a way to leapfrog VM, and stay permanently out in front."

"Okay, Brian," Laura said, turning to leave. "I know you guys all worked hard on this. I appreciate it. I'll sit down with it now and then leave you my thoughts on your BlackBerry."

Later that night, riding home in a cab, Brian got the e-mail from Laura with her reactions. Her reaction was not what he was expecting. She seemed to have read the report and concluded that Brian's team's recommendations were too risky.

Brian thought to himself, "I can't believe it! Laura is known as a risk-taker. It's what I love about her. What happened? We can do this!"

After thinking it over for a few minutes, Brian decided to write Laura this e-mail in response:

Laura—

Got your thoughts on the report. I *think* I understand where you are coming from, but I want to talk to you some more about this. I thought you would support the recommendations we made, and I'm disappointed that I have failed to convince you. I really think we have an opportunity here. With some bold action, we have the chance to cement our reputation early and possibly even lock out VM. We can't afford to play it safe. If you'll excuse the sports analogy, we've got to be like Ted Williams on the last day of the 1941 season. Williams was batting .39955, which would have rounded to a .400 season in the official statistics, and thus been a history-making achievement. His managers begged him not to play the last day of the season. They said, in essence, 'Why would you risk so much for so little?' Williams didn't agree. He wanted to be bold; so he played. He went six for eight in a doubleheader and finished the 1941 season at .406. And that's why we remember him decades later as one of the greatest players ever.

Can we talk tomorrow about trying to go six for eight?
Brian

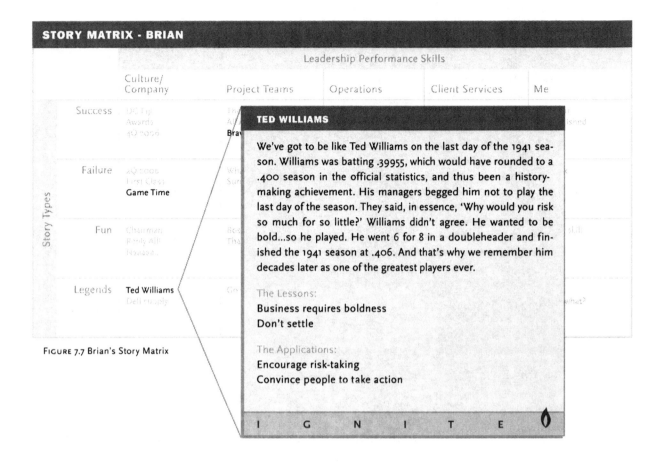

STORY MATRIX - BRIAN

Leadership Performance Skills

	Culture/ Company	Project Teams	Operations	Client Services	Me

Story Types

Success

Failure — Game Time

Fun

Legends — Ted Williams

TED WILLIAMS

We've got to be like Ted Williams on the last day of the 1941 season. Williams was batting .39955, which would have rounded to a .400 season in the official statistics, and thus been a history-making achievement. His managers begged him not to play the last day of the season. They said, in essence, 'Why would you risk so much for so little?' Williams didn't agree. He wanted to be bold...so he played. He went 6 for 8 in a doubleheader and finished the 1941 season at .406. And that's why we remember him decades later as one of the greatest players ever.

The Lessons:
Business requires boldness
Don't settle

The Applications:
Encourage risk-taking
Convince people to take action

I   G   N   I   T   E

Figure 7.7 Brian's Story Matrix

LEAD WITH STORIES

Like Brian in the story above, all leaders feel the crush of time and the pressure for results. We are pulled in many different directions, often without good preparation. We are exposed to more information than ever before, but not necessarily the information we need. And the stakes continue to get higher.

Leaders like Brian make daily choices about how to communicate important messages to their employees, peers, and bosses. And the performance of any organization depends on how well its leaders communicate. Performance is dictated by how each employee interprets and takes action on the communication received from leaders. Too often, leaders choose the most expedient, but ultimately more costly, method of communication.

"They say I tell a great many stories; I reckon I do, but I have found in the course of a long experience that common people, take them as they run, are more easily informed through the medium of a broad illustration than in any other way, and as to what the hypercritical few may think, I don't care."

— ABRAHAM LINCOLN

"At its most fundamental, Story provides a simple agent through which we can communicate complex meaning.... The great religions have all been based on pervasive and memorable stories that provide a common set of values and beliefs to their adherents. The stories provide role models and heuristics that allow members of religion to make choices in circumstances not anticipated by the original storyteller. The Christian Religion started with a highly ethical individual who conveyed his values through stories and parables. The theologians arrived some years later. Without the theologians the religion would not have 'scaled,' but without the storyteller nothing of value would have been created. One of the problems with much management science is that we too often start with the theologians and forget the storyteller."

– David Snowden[5]

In order to have the most impact on the business, leaders need to choose the tools that have the most leverage—less time spent with more impact and more effectiveness. In the situation outlined above, Brian told several stories that will have people thinking long after the hallway conversations and meetings are over.

By telling just a handful of well-placed stories throughout the course of a day, Brian created context where there was none. He painted a picture in his interactions and he gave people a reason to care. And because stories spread, it is likely that Julie, Kathy, Jose, Danny, and Laura will continue to benefit from his stories as they share them with others. In fact, it's likely that they will add those stories to their repertoire.

Stories work so efficiently as a leadership tool because they *put into motion* the right tactics and the right ways to think through decisions. We can read many books on leadership, but it is very hard to put these great ideas into motion. So we fail to execute. Stories are our means to execute because we all carry around a "starter set" of stories of success and failure. The Win Book and the Story Matrix expand this "starter set" into a rich, powerful repository of stories that help us lead.

These stories, in combination with other stories they may have heard or read, provide leaders with a very powerful, flexible tool set that they carry with them all the time, challenge to challenge, job to job, and out into their lives. It is the ability to have a good story at the ready and to go beyond the usual PowerPoint slides that makes all the difference.

CHAPTER 7:
SUMMARY

THE BITS AND BULLETS

- Leaders don't add more noise to the channel, they tell us stories to help us make sense of how to perform.

- Leaders encourage and influence us to tell our stories and thereby build more of an open-source environment where all of us can bring our best stuff.

- Be cognizant of the daily choices you are making with what you are communicating and how you are communicating it.

- Because stories carry context and successes and failures, they will travel farther and stick better.

THE PICTURES

Slide from Brian's PowerPoint Presentation

Slide from Susan's PowerPoint Presentation

Brian's Story Matrix with the **Game Time** Story in Detail

Brian's Story Matrix with the *Braveheart* Story in Detail

Brian's Story Matrix with the **Birthday Cake** Story in Detail

Brian's Story Matrix with the **Harvard Med School** Story in Detail

Brian's Story Matrix with the **Ted Williams** Story in Detail

THE STORIES

Game Time
Unethical behavior can and does happen

Braveheart
Strong teams can count on each other to always be there when needed

Birthday Cake
Having some fun and going above and beyond can reshape a client's perspective

Harvard Medical School
You will never have all the information you need at the time you need it

Ted Williams
Be bold and take risks

CHAPTER 7:
MY THOUGHTS AND IDEAS

CHAPTER 8:
SELLING STORIES

ATTENTION, PLEASE!

There is a good reason that a chapter on selling with stories follows a chapter on leadership. You may ask, "What does selling have to do with leadership?" The short answer is: everything. In many ways, leadership and selling are inseparable. Leadership *is* selling.

As leaders, our main role is to help our people and our organizations get somewhere. And often, it is up to us to define exactly what "somewhere" looks like and then *sell* why it's important for us to go there together. When Lou Gerstner got to IBM, it didn't take him too long to realize that the cold, reasoned analysis that he brought from McKinsey wasn't going to fly. So he changed his approach and began to hold face-to-face meetings with thousands of employees in which he directly sold the changes he was making.[2] And the results speak for themselves.

Similarly, as salespeople our job is to help our clients "get somewhere" with the use of our products and services. And in order to sell or convince anyone of anything, the first thing we need is their attention! Salespeople have the very same challenge other types of leaders do. They need to get someone focused on what they are saying long enough to have an impact on that person's decision-making process.

> "People are much more interested in hearing stories than in being sold on a product, and they are more likely to cast themselves in the plot."
>
> – RICHARD SAUL WURMAN[1]

We tend to define leadership as "executing strategy" or "getting results through people." This is no different from a salesperson's challenge. Selling is leadership. Salespeople, in order to accomplish the objectives of the organization, have to create a strategy. That strategy must have components that are very similar to that of other types of leaders. What are the end results I have to achieve? Whose help do I need? What can go wrong? What are the first few things I need to do? What are the risks to my strategy? And on and on.

Salespeople, like other leaders, don't have direct control over the entire process of achieving results. Sales leaders aren't the bosses of the people who are most critical to their success—customers. Competition is everywhere. The pressure for results is high. Clients and customers are busier than ever.

The most valuable commodity that a salesperson can acquire is attention. However we gain that attention, we must make the most of it. We have to cut through the noise, not add more noise. Adding more noise to the channel leaves too much of the outcome to chance.

> "There are only two things that separate success from failure in most organizations today: **1.** Invent stuff worth talking about. **2.** Tell stories about what you've invented."
>
> – SETH GODIN[3]

STORIES DIFFERENTIATE YOU

Once you've got someone's attention, you need to differentiate yourself. This is where many sales professionals fail. They rely more heavily on the bits and bullets of selling—product information—than on really helping clients visualize how this information will affect them. Clients want outcomes, not features. Talking about benefits is a start, but it doesn't go far enough. Clients want to hear that you've helped others get down this same road. They want you to describe the twists and turns in that road, so that they can see exactly how they will arrive safely.

Clients *know* there are bumps in that road, and selling features and product information doesn't address those bumps. This is where junior salespeople tend to struggle. Because they haven't been down the road themselves, they focus instead on the cool car the client will be riding in, when all that the client wants to do is arrive safely. If the bumps in the road aren't addressed, they inevitably come up later to derail a potential sale. Those bumps have to be addressed, and the best way to handle them is through stories.

This does not mean that product information should be ignored. Product information should be put in context so that clients and customers can sense how the product will impact them. The best way to bring this to life is through stories.

Whirlpool is a company that has figured this out. Several years ago, it designed and implemented a new training program for the people who are responsible for helping appliance dealers sell product to consumers. Whirlpool had found that the dealers and their salespeople were focusing too heavily on product information and statistics at the expense of results. So Whirlpool moved the trainers into a house, literally, where they lived together, ate together, and actually used the company's products.[5]

These young people, many of whom had never cooked for themselves (and probably rarely cleaned), started fending for themselves and thereby learning how to get stains out of clothes, clean the house, and even make dinner for the occasional Whirlpool executive who happened to visit. They came away from this experience with more than product knowledge. They came away with stories; stories about how to use the products to handle common challenges and what the strengths and weaknesses of the products were. These stories helped them train the dealers in a way that gave them a much stronger appreciation for the products and what they could do.

Ultimately, sales leaders want to be knowledgeable and able to help their clients tackle problems. In the process of doing that, they will get better results by helping clients cut through the noise and differentiating themselves. In that spirit, let's meet Lisa.

> "Stories (not ideas, not features, not benefits) are what spread from person to person."
>
> – SETH GODIN[4]

A SALES LEADERSHIP STORY: "A SPRINT TO THE FINISH"

Lisa backed out of the way as the door of the cab swung open and a guy literally jumped out and started running, obviously late. "Should have set that alarm a little earlier," she said to the cabbie as she got in the back, only to see another man settling in.

"Sorry," the man said, smiling at Lisa and getting back out. "I didn't see you getting in. I'll get the next one. No biggie."

"Oh, thanks." Lisa said. "Have a great day." Her cab pulled out into heavy traffic, and Lisa pulled out her cell phone and dialed home.

After a moment, Dave, Lisa's husband, picked up. "Dave, don't forget, I've got dinner with a client tonight, okay?" She paused, but there's no response. "Dave? Dave are you there?" Nothing. The call is disconnected. "Arrrgh! This phone drives me nuts!"

Her cab stopped in traffic, Lisa started to type a message to Dave when she saw a new e-mail on her BlackBerry:

Lisa—

That presentation you e-mailed me last night doesn't make sense. I see the new pricing for what we added, but we can't figure out why it would be that much more for just a few tweaks. Can you get back to me ASAP? Bob

"That's because, Bob, you didn't 'tweak' the deal, you changed it radically! Why is that so hard to understand?" Lisa said to her BlackBerry, only to get a puzzled look from the driver in his rear-view mirror.

Her cab pulled up to her building just as Sara, her boss, was arriving.

"Good morning," said Sara. "How are you?"

"I'm fine. Just multitasking as usual."

"Yeah, me too," said Sara, shaking her head. "Since when did a short car trip become an exercise in juggling? I don't remember the last time I just listened to the radio."

"Radio? What's that?"

Laughing, Sara said, "Oh well, at least we look cool juggling the world's burdens! See you at 8?"

"Yup, I'll be there. See you soon."

Lisa peeled away from Sara in the lobby and headed for the newspaper stand to grab juice and coffee. Firing up her calendar, she wrote a note back to her client, Bob, at MW:

Bob—

Got your message. Let's try to connect this morning. I need to explain what I sent over to you. Do you have ten minutes to talk? Thanks.
Lisa

A few minutes later, Jeremy, one of Lisa's junior colleagues, walked into to Lisa's office as she looked at her calendar. "Hey, partner," he said. "How goes it?"

"Doing fine. Just looking at what I've got going today. You?"

"Great," said Jeremy. "Got a question for you, though."

Looking up from her screen, Lisa asked, "Yeah? What is it?"

Jeremy pulled out a binder from the recent sales training session he attended and showed Lisa a PowerPoint slide. "See this page? This is a really helpful list of stuff we need to be doing and thinking. And when they talked about it in training, it really made sense. But I can't remember what some of these mean. How am I supposed to remember all of these?"

Loving Jeremy's enthusiasm, Lisa said, "Good question." But then she continued a bit too strongly. "You don't remember what they said in class?"

"Uh, not really," Jeremy said, embarrassed.

Lisa immediately felt bad for embarrassing him. "No, no, that's not what I meant. I mean, I'm not at all surprised that you don't remember. They wash a lot of information over you at those sessions."

"Man, that's for sure," he said, relieved. "I like the sessions a lot, it's just that if I'm going to get ahead, I need to remember it all."

"Jeremy, you are a champ for even thinking that. But realize: you can't take everything they say and become great at it overnight. Give yourself a chance, bud." She took a look at the PowerPoint slide. "So, which one of these is giving you the most trouble?"

Pointing to one of the bullet points on a slide entitled "10 Things High-Performing Salespeople Do" he said, "This one. 'Support Those Who Support You.' I guess they mean to just be nice to people you work with. But that's obvious."

She smiled again at Jeremy's genuine enthusiasm. "I think that's part of it. But you knew that already. In fact, you do that already. I think they are referring to something deeper."

"Like what?"

Lisa struggled to come up with an example. "You know what? I'm not sure. But let me think about it and get back to you. Is that alright?"

"Of course. We've got to go to the 8 o'clock meeting anyway. Thanks for the help. See you in a few minutes."

As Jeremy walked away, Lisa pulled out her Story Matrix and thought about how lucky BA was to have a couple of young salespeople like Jeremy.

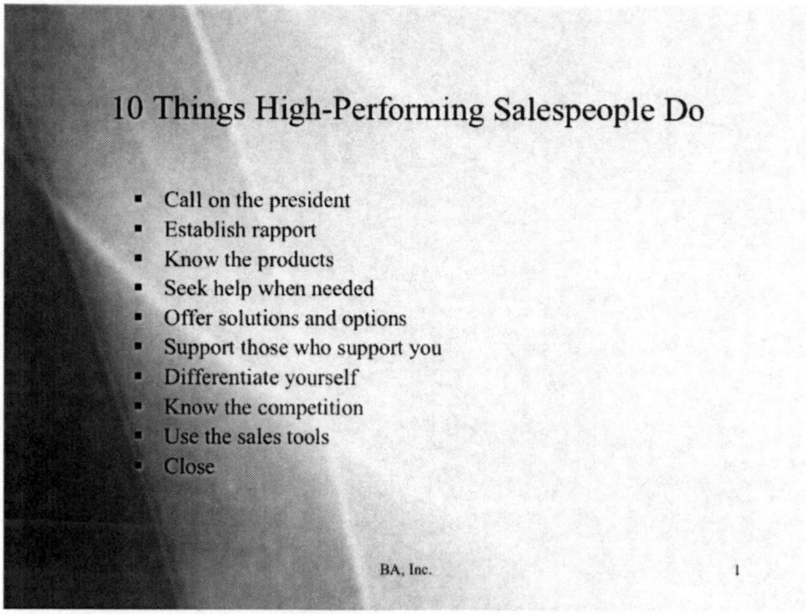

FIGURE 8.1 Slide from a Training PowerPoint Presentation

Sara kicked off the 8 AM weekly meeting of her seven-person sales team. "Morning, folks. Thanks for being on time. Okay, you know the drill. BlackBerrys off—unless you are expecting a baby." Everyone laughed as she continued. "I've looked over the combined sales pipeline and it's going to be a sprint to the finish this quarter. And I'm sure you agree with me. I'd much rather walk over the finish line than have to sprint. We got taken to task after missing our numbers last quarter, and I don't want that to happen again. Let's talk through our top five situations and figure out how to get them done, okay?" She pointed to her senior-most salesperson. "Walter, you're up."

Over the next hour, the team worked through their top-five list of client situations. Most of the give-and-take was standard fare—questions, reminders, a few suggestions—but very little innovative thinking. This bothered Sara and Lisa, as they were both feeling a lot of pressure to succeed. Sara knew that the rest of her team felt it too, but the discussion was not yielding any breakthrough ideas.

Walter, responding to another colleague's situation, said, "Scott, as you've said, there may be nothing more you can do to win that contract. It just seems that your competition is being pretty inflexible, given what your client told you about them. Even though our price is probably higher, there's got to be a way to take advantage of that inflexibility."

"I know. You are right," Scott said, stressed. "But my client, Randall, doesn't get that our solution is more robust than theirs. He's admitted that they are less flexible, but he's still so focused on the dollars and cents that I don't know if I will be able to sway him." He slapped the table in frustration. "I know I'm biased, but our solution is exactly what he needs, and he knows it!"

Sara paused, searching for an idea. "And you have explained to him all facets of our solution?"

"Yes! About ten times! You were there for most of that!"

Sara shook her head. "I know. I'm just looking for a way to break through to this guy."

"You and me both."

Lisa suddenly remembered a story she had read a couple of years ago. "This guy, Randall, sounds like the BMW owner in that story."

"Huh?" Scott replied, confused.

Remembering the details, Lisa said, "Yeah, he's just like that!"

Sara was getting impatient and looking at her watch. "Lisa, what are you talking about?"

"Oh, it's a legend I heard or read somewhere a while back. This guy who owned a fancy BMW took it in for service one day. And, as is custom, the Beemer dealership gave him a loaner to use. A few days later, the guy comes back to pick up his car and while he's driving it home, he notices that the service guys forgot to replace the ash tray. See, they wash the cars before they give them back to the customers as a feature of the service. But they forgot to replace the ash tray. So the guy calls the dealership from the car and tells them. Their response is, 'We're really sorry, sir. You can swing back in any time and we will replace your ash tray.' The driver hangs up, but now he's mad. He's already miles away from the dealership, and it's going to be a pain to go back and get it. Because it's their mistake, he thinks that they ought to bring it to him. He's gets so wound up about it, he calls the local Lexus dealer, just to see what they would do in the same situation. He explains what happened to the Lexus service technician who picked up the phone, and he asks, 'What would you do in that situation?' The service tech says, 'Sir, we would bring the ash tray to your home and replace it.' Just as the driver is thinking to himself, 'Of course, that would be his answer,' the service tech says, 'Sir, may I ask you a question? Which BMW dealership do you go to? I'll have one of my technicians swing by there right now, pick up your ash tray, and bring it to your home and install it.'

STORY MATRIX - LISA

		Leadership Performance Skills					
		Culture/ Planning	Execution	Follow-through	Presentations	Teamwork	Me
Story Types	Success	Jump how high?	Singapore Sling	Lava Lamp	Recovery	$104,000 Wingman	Analyze... synthesize
	Failure	Greedy 95 slides "3 prong strategy"	Rotten berries BA Day				
	Fun	"That's it!"	Nanno'no				
	Legends	Random Walk	Car Dealer				

FIGURE 8.2 Lisa's Story Matrix

CAR DEALER

This guy who owned a fancy BMW took it in for service one day. When he picks it up, he notices that the service guys forgot to replace the ash tray. So the guy calls the dealership from the car and tells them. Their response is; 'We're really sorry, sir. You can swing back in any time and we will replace your ash tray.' He gets so mad that he calls the local Lexus dealer. He explains what happened to the Lexus service technician and asks; 'What would you do in that situation?' The service tech says; 'Sir, we would bring the ash tray to your home and replace it.' Then the guy says; 'Sir, may I ask you a question? Which BMW dealership do you go to? I'll have one of my technicians swing by there right now, pick up your ash tray and bring it to your home and install it...'

The Lessons:
We are always selling
Go above and beyond
Break out of the usual behaviors

The Applications:
Build client delight
Drive superior customer service
Empower your front lines

I   G   N   I   T   E

"Whoa!" Jeremy said, shocked. "That's what I'm talkin' about!"

"Did that really happen?" Scott asked, smiling.

"I think so," said Lisa. "I'm not sure, really. But your situation reminded me of this guy's predicament."

"That is his situation," said Scott "and we are the Lexus dealer." Scott was getting excited. "I'm going to tell Randall that story."

Sara was skeptical. "Not so fast. We don't ever disparage the competition."

Scott responded, "I'm not going to. But that's the perfect story. It's not about disparaging the competition at all. It's about showing him how we will go above and beyond for him!"

As the meeting broke up, Jeremy caught up with Lisa in the hallway. "I loved that story!" he said, smiling ear to ear.

"Thanks. I wrote that story down a couple of years ago when I first came across it and it just popped back into my head."

"What's so cool about that story is that it helped Scott, but it also helps me understand a couple of other things."

"Oh yeah?" Lisa said, enthusiastically. "Like what?"

"Well, one of the bullet points on that slide I showed you earlier is something like 'Differentiate Yourself.' That story is a perfect example of what to remember when you are trying to differentiate yourself—you have to look for opportunities to surprise customers in a positive way. That Lexus guy could have just said, 'No, that would never happen here,' and left it at that. It also makes me think that we need to be very careful with clients and not drop the ball, because someone else could always pick it up."

"I hadn't thought of those things, but you are right," she said, impressed. "So, back to your question from this morning, as long as I'm on a roll. I thought of an illustration for you of how to support those around you or whatever that bullet point was."

"Great. Bring it on!"

"A year or so ago, I was in a very competitive situation with a new client we were trying to win. The client was incredibly demanding, and just when it looked like we had given them all the information we could, they would demand more. It sent me and everyone around me jumping through hoops. We reconfigured our pricing, the solution, the team. We stayed up nights rewriting the proposal. We met with the client to explain all of the changes, and then he would ask for more. It was a nightmare. Luckily, the story has a happy ending. We won the business. And, of course, I thanked the team up and down for the hard work. But I also needed a way to connect their hard work to something real. So I went to Accounts Receivable and asked Rick for a big favor. Rick is the guy who receives the checks from our clients. I asked him to call me when that check came in. So, a month or so later, he called to tell me that the client had made the first payment of $104,000. I called a meeting of the team that had worked on winning that deal. When we had everyone together, I asked them to stand in a circle. They,

STORY MATRIX - LISA

| | | Leadership Performance Skills | | | | | |
		Culture/ Planning	Execution	Follow-through	Presentations	Teamwork	Me
Story Types	Success	Jump how high?	Singapore Sling	Lava Lamp	Recovery	$104,000	Analyze, synthesize
	Failure	Greedy 95 slides "3 prong strategy"	Rotten berries BA Day				
	Fun	"That's it!"	Jump, etc.				
	Legends	Bando in wall	Car Dealer				

FIGURE 8.3 Lisa's Story Matrix

$104,000

After a long struggle, we ended up winning a deal with a tough client. I thanked the team up and down for the hard work. But I also needed a way to connect their hard work to something real. So I went to Accounts Receivable and asked them to call me when that check came in. It came in, and I called a meeting of the team that had worked on winning that deal. I asked them to stand in a circle. They, of course, thought I was nuts, but they did it. I re-told the story of how we had won that deal and how hard everyone had worked. And then I passed the check around. Now, most people have never held a check for $104,000 before! It was so cool, because not only were they stunned by the size of the check, I got to help them realize that their work created that money. That little meeting is one of the best successes I've had.

The Lessons:
Connect what people do day-to-day with the outcomes
Find additional ways to say 'thank-you'

The Applications:
Build more dedicated resources
Share successes
Reinforce great behavior
Empower your front lines

I   G   N   I   T   E

of course, thought I was nuts, but they did it. I retold the story of how we had won that deal and how hard everyone had worked. And then I passed the check around. Now, most people have never held a check for $104,000 before! It was so cool, because not only were they stunned by the size of the check, I got to help them realize that their work created that money. That little meeting is one of the best successes I've had."

"You are two for two!" Jeremy said, shaking his head.

"Ha! Thanks," Lisa said, laughing. "I just thought that might help put some meat back on the bones of those 'high-performance' bullet points!" Lisa looked at her watch. "Oh, man, I'm late. Gotta run to a client meeting across town. See you later!"

As Lisa sat in a cab on the way to a meeting with a potential client, she reviewed BA's new service approach called the "Fish Bone." She liked the new approach, and thought that it should be easy to explain because it was laid out on a slide in the form of a fish bone, with each 'bone' making up a unique service offering.

A little while later, Lisa was confidently clicking through the middle of her presentation to Jennifer, a senior leader at HT. "So, as you can see, these offerings fit together to give you a comprehensive solution."

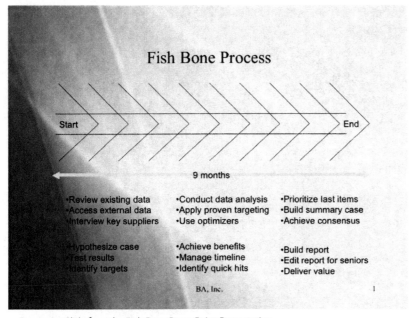

FIGURE 8.4 Slide from the Fish Bone PowerPoint Presentation

"Lisa, with all due respect, this looks like overkill," Jennifer said, frowning. "I think I see what BA is trying to do, but this is way more than we need right now. Looks to me like you guys are pricing yourselves right out of the market."

"Really? No, you don't understand. I mean, I haven't explained this well," Lisa said, sputtering. "Let me outline again why I think this makes sense for you and HT." She recovered a little. "This 'fish bone' approach is designed to anticipate your needs as our relationship grows. I didn't mean to imply that you buy all of this up front." Seeing some daylight, she continued. "It's simply pieces of the solution that get added as we go along. Does this make more sense?"

Jennifer was hesitant. "Uh, sort of. Are you saying that these services come 'a la carte'?"

"Yes. That's a great way to think about it," she said, smiling.

"I guess that makes sense, but this 'fish bone' thing looks too complex," Jennifer said while shaking her head. "I'll tell you right now that my people won't like it. They much prefer a simple, clean solution and BA seems to be heading in the opposite direction."

Lisa was deflated. "I'm sorry about that. I know that's not our intention, and I just don't think I've done justice to this new approach."

"Well, I've got to run to another meeting," Jennifer said, looking at her watch. "My team and I are scheduled to talk about this when we come back from the trade show in two weeks. Why don't you call me after the first of the month and I'll let you know what decision we've made?"

Lisa ran into Walter as she walked back into the office after her meeting at HT.

"Hey there, good meeting this morning. I liked your ideas," said Walter. "You coming back from HT?"

"Unfortunately, yes. Not pretty," Lisa said, looking dejected.

"What do you mean? During this morning's 'top five' you said that you were building a good relationship with the senior person there, and that they may be a possible near-term close."

"Ha! That meeting seems like years ago. No, the meeting couldn't have gone worse. Let's put it this way: I swerved out of control, crashed into a tree on the side of the road, recovered briefly, only to drive off a cliff on the other side of the road. Does that give you a mental picture?"

"Uh, yeah," said Walter, not sure what to say. "Sounds brutal. Weren't you going to show her the new fish bone thing?"

"Oh yeah, and I choked on the fish bone."

"Bummer. That new approach looks good. What went wrong?"

"Honestly, I don't know. I explained it just like it had been explained to me. I thought she would love it, and I couldn't have been more wrong. She thought it was overblown and complicated."

Jeremy and Sara came up as Walter walked away for another appointment.

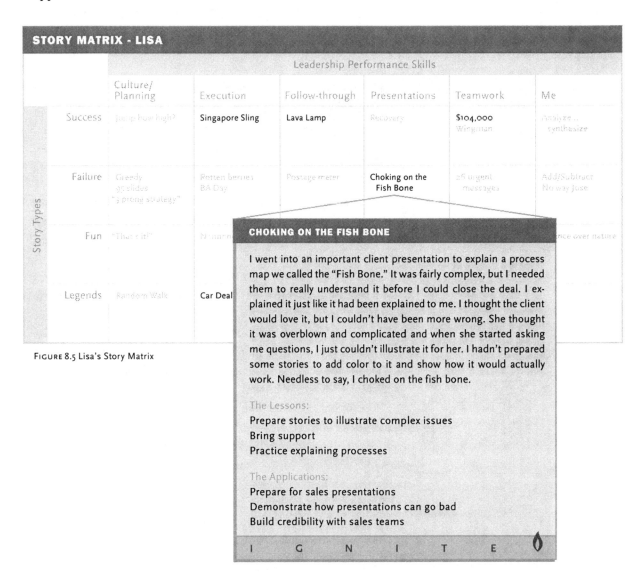

FIGURE 8.5 Lisa's Story Matrix

STORY MATRIX - LISA

Leadership Performance Skills

Story Types		Culture/ Planning	Execution	Follow-through	Presentations	Teamwork	Me
	Success	Jump how high?	Singapore Sling	Lava Lamp	Recovery	$104,000 Wingman	Analyze & synthesize
	Failure	Greedy 95 slides "3 prong strategy"	Rotten berries BA Day	Postage meter	Choking on the Fish Bone	25 urgent messages	Add/Subtract No way Jose
	Fun	"That's it!"					nce over nature
	Legends	Random Walk	Car Deal				

CHOKING ON THE FISH BONE

I went into an important client presentation to explain a process map we called the "Fish Bone." It was fairly complex, but I needed them to really understand it before I could close the deal. I explained it just like it had been explained to me. I thought the client would love it, but I couldn't have been more wrong. She thought it was overblown and complicated and when she started asking me questions, I just couldn't illustrate it for her. I hadn't prepared some stories to add color to it and show how it would actually work. Needless to say, I choked on the fish bone.

The Lessons:
Prepare stories to illustrate complex issues
Bring support
Practice explaining processes

The Applications:
Prepare for sales presentations
Demonstrate how presentations can go bad
Build credibility with sales teams

I   G   N   I   T   E

Preempting the obvious question from Sara, Lisa said, "Yes, I met with HT. No, it did not go well."

Sara was surprised. "Oh, no. You were so confident about that one."

"Well, I spoke too soon. Sara, I'm sorry. I'm going to have to dig deep to find another opportunity."

"Wait a minute. Are you telling me you lost that one?" Sara was not pleased. "Is HT no longer an opportunity?"

"I don't think so. Even if they are, they certainly won't come in before next quarter. Jennifer all but told me not to hold my breath."

"Lisa, I'm sorry to hear that." Sara was calm, but not ready to give up. "I know it's painful, but I need to know exactly what happened. Our whole quarter is at risk and I was, we were, counting on HT to come through. Can we talk about it?"

Lisa was suddenly tired. "Sure. But just remember, I've still got to put the finishing touches on that big presentation to Carl Hunter at RK tonight. If we can get that deal, we will be in great shape."

Lisa and Sara walked to Sara's office to discuss HT. On the way, Lisa invited Jeremy to listen in. She recounted the meeting for Sara and Jeremy.

Lisa finished her recap. "So, that's pretty much it. You two have both seen the proposal I had on the table for HT. I thought that making her aware of the new approach would only help my case, and it looks like I've dug a nice, deep hole for myself."

Sara was frustrated. "Damn. It's not our policy to add features to our solution that hurt us. They are supposed to help us close more business!"

Lisa agreed, "Amen to that."

"I have a question," Jeremy suddenly spoke up. "You know how you two always say, 'Don't just sell features, sell benefits?'"

"Sure. Of course," Lisa said. "I walked her through the benefits."

"No, that's not my question," Jeremy said. "This approach is totally new. So, we don't really know the benefits; we only think we know what they will be. It sounds like what this Jennifer might need is a story that describes how several of the 'bones' of the new approach might help her team. If we can help her *see* that, even if it's hypothetical, it seems like it might help simplify our whole proposal."

Lisa looked at Sara. "This guy is good, you know."

Nodding, Sara said, "That's why we hired him." She looked at Jeremy. "Jeremy, that's a great thought. Lisa, I think you should take this advice. Why don't you write something up for Jennifer along the lines of what Jeremy suggests, and get it right over to her? It may help your cause."

"Will do. I'm on it."

Back at her desk, Lisa checked her e-mail and saw a message from Bob Durham at MW. She decided to call him immediately and check if she could meet him face to face. She didn't want to risk a bad outcome by sending him another e-mail.

Lisa hung up with Bob's assistant. "Great. I'll be right over. Tell him thanks!"

On her way over, Lisa thought through how she would explain the revised pricing to Bob, and why the "tweaks" he made were substantial changes. She decided to take some of Jeremy's advice and walk Bob through a real client story, outlining for him how the changes he made to the proposal actually worked for another client, and how even though it was a bigger project, the client was well-served.

Finishing her client story in Bob's office, Lisa said, "When it was all said and done, the client was able to get through implementation faster, even though it was a bigger project. Bob, in fact, I'd be happy to connect you to this client. He's a great guy, and you could get his perspective."

"Thanks for the offer," Bob said, nodding. "This is a lot clearer to me now. I'll walk my team through that story and I'm sure they will get it. I'll call you if I have other questions. And I appreciate the offer to connect with your client, but I don't think I need it now."

"No problem. Yes, do call if you need any clarification. When do you think you'll be able to talk with your team?"

Bob thought for a moment. "At tomorrow's staff meeting. You know this is a high priority for us."

"Great," Lisa said, relieved. "So, do I owe you anything?"

"Not that I can think of, no."

Lisa got up to leave. "So, where's your beloved orange Lava Lamp that you always have on your desk?"

Bob chuckled and then pretended to wipe tears away from his eyes. "My...lamp...broke. I turned to get the phone and sent it flying across the room. This office will never be the same."

As Lisa walked out of Bob's office building, she saw a Target store across the street and had an idea. She ran in and bought a $12 Lava Lamp, and then drove back across to Bob's office.

"Bob, I couldn't stand to see you so sad," she said, walking back into his office with a gift bag.

Bob looked up, surprised to see her. "What the..." Opening the bag and pulling out the Lava Lamp, he said, "Holy moly! It's the '70s again! Excellent!" Bob laughed and held up the lamp. "You are the best! I got my Lava Lamp back!"

"It was just too tragic, too heart-wrenching. I had to do something!"

"Seriously, thanks," he said. "You know how that lamp is just my way of keeping a little revolution alive in a Dilbert world! And guess what? You're pretty clever. I'll think of you every time I look at it."

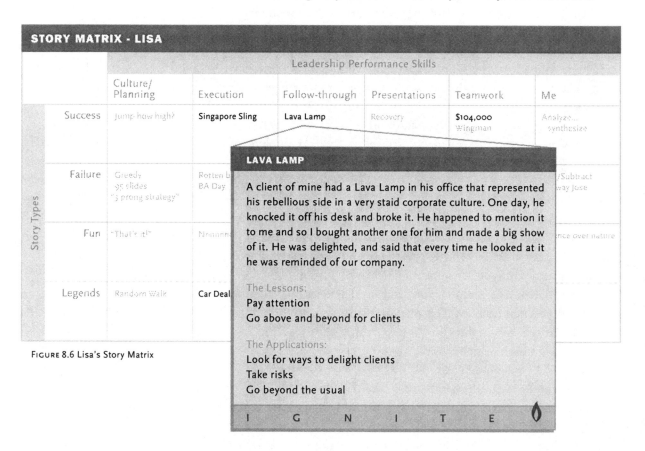

FIGURE 8.6 Lisa's Story Matrix

STORY MATRIX - LISA

		Leadership Performance Skills					
		Culture/ Planning	Execution	Follow-through	Presentations	Teamwork	Me
Story Types	Success	Jump- how high?	Singapore Sling	Lava Lamp	Recovery	$104,000 Wingman	Analyze... synthesize
	Failure	Greedy 95 slides "3 prong strategy"	Rotten b... BA Day				/Subtract way jose
	Fun	"That's it"	Nnnnnn...				nce over nature
	Legends	Random Walk	Car Deal				

LAVA LAMP

A client of mine had a Lava Lamp in his office that represented his rebellious side in a very staid corporate culture. One day, he knocked it off his desk and broke it. He happened to mention it to me and so I bought another one for him and made a big show of it. He was delighted, and said that every time he looked at it he was reminded of our company.

The Lessons:
Pay attention
Go above and beyond for clients

The Applications:
Look for ways to delight clients
Take risks
Go beyond the usual

I   G   N   I   T   E

As she rode back to the office, Lisa's smile turned to a frown as she remembered the presentation she needed to finish before her dinner meeting.

Jeremy walked into a conference room where Lisa has been at work for several hours. "Uh, did a paper factory explode in here?"

Lisa looked up, not smiling. "Arrgh."

"You've got that meeting at RK tonight, right? Need help?"

Lisa lightened up. "You, my friend, are a good man. Not too bright, but a good man."

Jeremy laughed. "Well, you know what they say, a friend in need..."

"...is a pain in the backside," Lisa finished. "That I am. Actually, I know it doesn't look like it, but there's really not that much to do. I've got to be over there in an hour, and I just have to revise this timeline page, print, and bind five copies." She added, sarcastically, "Carl was kind enough to tell me 45 minutes ago that he's bringing four of his folks to the meeting."

"Just give me what's finished, and I'll start copying for you."

"Can we clone you? Thanks, J. I owe you big time."

Jeremy grabbed the finished documents. "No you don't," he said, as he walked out.

Lisa got back to work revising the timeline. Jeremy was gone a long time, and Lisa was starting to wonder what happened to him.

Jeremy frowned as he walked back into the conference room. "Uh, you are not going to believe this."

Lisa looked up quickly. "What?"

"Both copiers are down. One is jammed and the other one is off, and I don't have the code to turn it on. I went downstairs to security and they wouldn't let me in any other office to make the copies."

Lisa was now getting seriously stressed. "Please tell me you're joking."

"I wish. Lisa, I guess I can ride the elevator and look for an office that's still open!"

"We don't have time! I'll never make it to a Kinko's in time to copy and bind five presentations! I figured that you would have them done when you got back and we would just slip in the last page."

"Sorry."

"Jeremy, it's not your fault," she said, trying to think. "I just can't show up empty-handed. Carl will be frustrated. I knew I should have finished this last night!"

"Wait. Wait a minute," Jeremy said, closing his eyes. "Idea coming on. Yes, got it! Here's what you'll do. Stop at an office supply store on the way to dinner. Buy five 'thumb' drives. You know, those little USB drives. They're super cheap now. Bring your laptop and just put the presentation on the thumb drives and hand those out to everyone. They will think you are so cool! You can just walk them through it on your laptop *and* you haven't wasted any paper!"

Lisa was nearly speechless. "That...is beautiful. Jeremy, I don't know what to say. You are a genius. Thank you."

"Go forth to victory!" he said, in a mock deep voice.

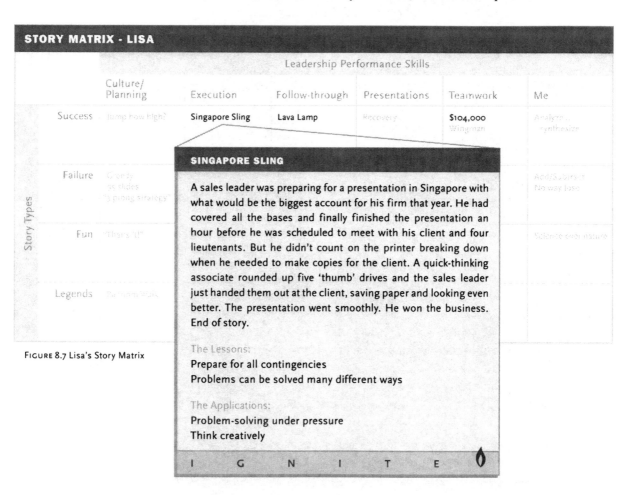

FIGURE 8.7 Lisa's Story Matrix

Forty-five minutes later, Lisa was at dinner with five people from RK, moving into the middle of her presentation. "Kristen, it looks like you have a question."

Kristen, one of Carl's lieutenants, referred to a feature that Lisa had just described. "I do. I think I'm tracking how this all fits together at a high level, but I'm lost in the details. Can you explain how this actually works?"

"Sure," Lisa said. "The best way to illustrate how this comes together is to tell a quick story of how another client of ours is putting this to use. Is that okay?"

Carl jumped in. "Sure. Go ahead."

Lisa told a story about a West Coast client that showed the group how they would actually use the tools. Wrapping up the story, she said, "So, I do have to tell you about an important lesson we learned, though."

Kristen was curious. "What's that?"

"Well, it was a timing issue. Because all of these pieces fit closely together, we had to stay on top of timing. What happened with this client is that we ended up turning on the tracking capability just one day before they were ready. They immediately started getting calls from confused customers, until we discovered the problem. Luckily, we caught it quickly and only several customers were affected. It was our fault, but it taught us an important lesson. And now we have a specific process document that must be signed off before we turn that feature on."

Kristen was impressed. "Lisa, I appreciate you telling us that part."

"Well, it was a good learning for us. But what doesn't kill you makes you stronger. What is it that Warren Buffett says? 'A rising tide lifts all boats. Until the tide goes out, and you find out who's naked!'"

"Yes, I heard that once!" Carl said, laughing.

Lisa was also laughing. "Our job is to make sure that when the tide goes out, we're all covered!"

SELL THE TRUTH

Natalie Goldberg, in her phenomenal book, *Writing Down the Bones*, tells of a rabbi friend of hers who wasn't allowed to take notes during his rabbinical training.[6] All of the students were to

"Humans are too smart to be fooled by a Potemkin village, a facade that pretends to be one thing and turns out to be another. Sure, you can fool some people once or twice, but this is the key lesson of the new marketing: once fooled, a person will never repeat your story to someone else. If you are not authentic, you will get the benefit of just one sale, not a hundred. The cost of your deception is too high."

– Seth Godin[7]

listen to the lectures, stories, and discussions and they were expected to know the material—with no notes. Imagine how different that would be. Imagine walking into your next sales presentation and saying, "Hey everybody, just listen. Don't take notes. You won't need notes." There is no way that approach could succeed if you used slides with bits and bullets. Stories would have to make up a large percentage of your presentation, or no one would remember what you said.

That's why this is what you should be doing anyway. Make no mistake, a story is not a substitute for rigor. Salespeople cannot afford to just tell stories and hope for the best. We must have our heads around the product information, features, benefits, and the nuances of the client situation. We must manage the sales process closely, from prospecting to closing to implementation. But that's the price of getting in the game. In order to excel, we need to weave these disparate elements together into stories that make our solutions come alive.

One of the best ways to ensure that you are going beyond bits and bullets is to ask: What will make my presentation stick? What will make the client talk about it after I've walked out of the office?

One of the things that our heroine Lisa is dealing with in the story above is how fast everyone is moving. She and her team are rushing to turn in a strong quarter. Her clients are just as busy, juggling commitments, proposals, and people. Attention is at a premium.

"The power to influence is often associated with force, the ability to make someone do what you want them to do. That suggests a push strategy. However, story is a pull strategy—more like a powerful magnet than a bulldozer."

– Annette Simmons[8]

Her stories slowed down the action. She gave her colleagues and her clients a chance to breathe. They could pause for a minute or two and receive something that enlightens them instead of another fact or product feature that has to get crammed into their head somewhere between the conference room number for their next meeting and the due date for their next report.

Salespeople are rarely able to reach all of the decision makers at once. This is where stories are also useful, because they more readily spread from client to client. It is much easier for clients to remember a story that illustrates your product than the technical specifications of that product. Thus, it is much easier for them to relate the story to their peers. As salespeople, we can start the ball rolling with stories, and we can offer our clients something that sticks.

CHAPTER 8:
SUMMARY

THE BITS AND BULLETS

- Leaders must define where the organization is going, and then "sell" why it's important for everyone to go there together.

- Stories help leaders gain the precious attention of their audiences and thereby improve chances for success.

- Clients and our own people want to see the "whole story" —including the successes and failures—so they can make well-informed decisions.

- Use stories to rise above the "chatter" of product information and truly differentiate yourself.

- Approach your presentations as if your clients or people will not be allowed to take notes or refer to any documentation.

THE PICTURES

Slide from a Training PowerPoint Presentation

Lisa's Story Matrix with the **Car Dealer** Story in Detail

Lisa's Story Matrix with the **$104,000** Story in Detail

Slide from the Fish Bone PowerPoint Presentation

Lisa's Story Matrix with the **Choking on the Fish Bone** Story in Detail

Lisa's Story Matrix with the **Lava Lamp** Story in Detail

Lisa's Story Matrix with the **Singapore Sling** Story in Detail

THE STORIES

Car Dealer

Great sales leaders look for opportunities to do something unique for a client

$104,000

Connect your people to the drivers of the business and how they personally have an impact on them

Choking on the Fish Bone

We must carry stories that actually illustrate how we get results

Lava Lamp

Find different ways to connect with busy clients beyond the usual brochures and e-mails

Singapore Sling

Think outside the box when faced with a difficult situation

Chapter 8:
MY THOUGHTS AND IDEAS

CHAPTER 9:

MOTIVATIONAL STORIES

"Analysis might excite the mind but it hardly offers a route to the heart. And that is where leaders have to go if they are to motivate people to launch transformational change and spark rapid action with energy and enthusiasm. Now that most managers are being called upon to tackle the challenges of leadership, they are discovering what great leaders have instinctively known all along: it is stories that inspire and persuade."

– STEPHEN DENNING[1]

GIVING GIFTS

Wouldn't it be great if we could motivate and inspire people every day? We can. We can break through the noise and give people the gift of story. Why not be a leader that gives these gifts? That's what stories are; they are gifts.

Sometimes inspirational stories are stories of extraordinary accomplishment and sometimes they are just plain old stories told at the right time. Leaders often assume that to motivate their teams or inspire people they have to do something completely unexpected or out of this world. Not so. People respond to authentic leadership, and that means telling your stories and theirs. They don't have to be stories of climbing Mt. Everest or going over Niagara Falls in a barrel. They can be common stories of regular people tackling challenges—told at the right time. I've seen a plain old story motivate a group simply because it gave them a chance to sit still for a second and reflect on what's important to them.

We are all on a hero's journey. It's called life. And as we all know intimately, this journey is fraught with excitement and peril, with ups and downs and victories and defeats. Motivating and inspiring people is "reaching through" to them. When a leader reaches

"Great leaders discover what is universal and capitalize on it. Their job is to rally people toward a better future. Leaders can succeed in this only when they can cut through differences of race, sex, age, nationality, and personality and, using stories and celebrating heroes, tap into those very few needs we all share."

– Marcus Buckingham[2]

"I suspect that if we change the stories people hear every day, we could change the world."

– David Holt and Bill Mooney[3]

"At a time when corporate survival often requires disruptive change, leadership involves inspiring people to act in unfamiliar, and often unwelcome, ways. Mind-numbing cascades of numbers or daze-inducing PowerPoint slides won't achieve this goal. Even the most logical arguments usually won't do the trick. But effective storytelling often does."

– Stephen Denning[5]

through, it means that leader cuts through the normal day-to-day motions we all go through to connect to something that is timeless. It may be one of the most difficult and most rewarding things that leaders do.

Think about a time when you were truly inspired. You felt great. Suddenly, things were crystal clear. The noise and the interference were stripped away to reveal something true. You saw possibilities. You felt excitement. One of the reasons for these feelings is that they *are* feelings. Motivation and inspiration come from the emotions. It is the rare person that can analyze her way to inspiration. When we are inspired, we feel it at a deep, emotional level; not an intellectual level. And that is why stories are such a powerful tool to motivate and inspire. They can use the data but go beyond it to persuade with emotion. In a *Harvard Business Review* article entitled "Storytelling That Moves People," Hollywood screenwriting coach Robert McKee says that even if leaders manage to persuade, "you've done so only on an intellectual basis. That's not good enough, because people are not inspired to act by reason alone."[4]

Your stories can connect to both the heart and the mind. When the heart is engaged, it can convince the mind of anything.

So, what kinds of stories inspire? Stories that truly inspire are those that connect to our core values. We all want love, security, a reason to exist, a reason to laugh. When an inspirational story is told, it weaves its way into our core by connecting to and igniting an emotional reaction. We lose ourselves in the story and we become part of it.

Why not create some emotional reactions once in a while instead of spending all of our time brokering information? As leaders, we already spend a tremendous amount of our time as a broker of information. We filter the information that comes in, translate it, add to it, and send it out. Why not do the same with motivation and inspiration? Be a conduit for these stories. Collect these stories as you collect other types of data.

Chances are good that these things that motivate and inspire you also inspire those around you. And why not share that inspiration? Every culture, every organization, and every person carries around stories that truly inspire.

CHOOSING "MOTIVATION" STORIES

What types of "motivation" challenges do you face? Here are just a few big ones:

- Pushing a team to stretch to make their goals
- Rebuilding a team after a setback or loss
- Building excitement around a new strategy
- Getting a group fired up before a final push

In addition to stories that connect to our core values and concerns, there are several other questions to ask of your stories in order to ensure that they motivate and inspire:

- **Does the story help people bond together?** One of the great things about organizations is that they are teams. They can't help it. Organizations are just a bunch of people trying to climb a mountain together. Yes, some people may be better climbers and some are better map-readers, but everyone is playing a role. One of the things stories can do is acknowledge that fact. It's too easy to lose sight of the fact that we are on a team where other people are just trying to do the best they can. Reminding people that they have help, that other people are pulling for them and that this team is going to stick together goes a long way.

- **Does the story create a path to possibility?** Stories that inspire are ones where hardship was overcome, good arose out of bad, or an unexpected surprise brought a tremendous benefit. All of these stories help us understand that the future can be better than the past and the present. In fact, these types of stories help us make it so by showing the path to the future.

- **Does the story allow for some fun?** Of course, not all stories that motivate have to be fun. Some of the best motivational stories are gripping personal dramas. But, unless you are a stand-up comedian, you could probably use some levity in your workday. Stories that point out our foibles in a funny way or that highlight the elements of business that are truly crazy or bizarre can be very energizing. It helps us remember that it's just a job after all!

A MOTIVATIONAL LEADERSHIP STORY: "UP, DOWN, ALL AROUND"

Chris ducked back out of the cab and into the street, embarrassed that he hadn't noticed the woman getting in the other side. "You have a great day too," he said as he closed the door and the cab

> "...most executives struggle to communicate, let alone inspire. Too often, they get lost in the accoutrements of company speak: PowerPoint slides, dry memos, and hyperbolic missives from the corporate communications department. Even the most carefully researched and considered efforts are routinely greeted with cynicism, lassitude, or outright dismissal."
>
> – ROBERT MCKEE[6]

> "We understand ourselves through stories, by making stories out of our lives. Storytellers give people structure with which they can begin to look at their own lives and try to make sense of them. With all the noise we have in this culture, it's heartening that one person talking can still command attention."
>
> – DAVID HOLT AND BILL MOONEY[7]

crept out into traffic. Luckily for him, there was another pulling up. Chris jumped in.

A few minutes later, Chris dashed into his client's building and decided to grab a quick cup of coffee. Waiting in line, Chris pulled out his phone and dialed a colleague, Rod, in his office.

"Rod, I'll be over there in less than ten minutes. I had to drop something off over here. Just grabbing a coffee, then a cab back." Chris listened as Rod was clearly agitated. "No, I said I'd be there in less than ten minutes! Can't it wait?" Chris said. Then, "She said what? Oh, please. I can't believe it. Rod, please just sit tight. I'll be there in ten. You want a coffee? Rod? Rod?"

Juggling his case and two large coffees, Chris walked into his office at 7:28 AM. He headed for Rod's office and walked straight into the eye of a storm.

Kara, another of Chris's colleagues was intense. "Rod, once again, you are making assumptions that are...not right. If you continue to insist..."

"That's not fair, and you know it!" Rod said, leaning forward on his desk and interrupting. Pointing at Kara, he said, "I am simply trying to..."

Chris interrupted. "Time out. Time out please. Can somebody tell me what the hell is going on?"

Rod and Kara started talking at the same time. "We have...," said Rod, waving at Kara in frustration. "Go ahead. Be my guest."

Kara was shaking her head. "Look, Chris, both Rod and I got an e-mail from KM early this morning and we seem to have two completely different takes on it."

Chris suddenly got nervous because KM is the business partner whose software underlies RJ's ability to deliver its services to customers. "What does the e-mail say?"

Rod handed a printout of the e-mail to Chris. Nervous glances were exchanged as Chris read the note.

Chris looked up slowly. "Oh, great. Guys, this could be very, very bad. Have either of you talked to Sam over there?"

Rod was snide. "Obviously, we are still just trying to figure out what this means!"

"Okay, right. Let's talk about this. I'm not sure what he means either." Chris tried to lighten the mood by handing a coffee to both Kara and Rod. "Here, have a cold coffee," he said, as he looked at the e-mail again. "Sam says here, 'Due to some bad information from your group, our development team made decisions that have resulted in a product that we cannot support. Had we stuck with the original plan, and not changed it based on your information, we would be ready for the launch. Now, we are perhaps as much as two months out. One thing is clear: we need better communications.'" Chris started to put the pieces together and, as he figured it out, he was blunt. "So, you two are fighting over who gave Sam's development folks the wrong information?"

Carefully, Kara said, "Yes, sort of."

"That's pretty much it," agreed Rod.

Chris looked at his watch and was getting angry as he remembered that he had to be on a conference call at 8 AM. "Well, we can sit here all day and point fingers, or we can figure out what to do," he said a bit too harshly. "Which would you rather do?"

Rod extended an olive branch. "Look, I'm sure I made some mistakes here. Because I'm Sam's main contact, I've got to call him. Help me here. What do I say? If we miss this launch, we're screwed."

Kara met him halfway. "Rod, we are all responsible for this. We need to talk to Jill before we can respond anyway, so that should be our first course of action."

Chris was nodding, but still upset. "Talk to Jill," he said, turning to walk out of Rod's office. "Please loop back with me at 9, and please stay on the same team."

Chris thought about how much money the company stood to lose if they missed the launch of the new services as he walked down the hall to his office. He was so distracted that it took him three tries to correctly punch in the numbers for the conference bridge for his 8 AM call.

Eddie, one of Chris's managers, heard the beep. "Who just joined the circus? Chris, is that you?"

"Yeah. I'm here," Chris said, plowing past the usual niceties. "I've got a hard stop at 9, so let's get going."

Eddie was surprised. "Okay. Well, Raj is here and we've got Lindsay, Al, and Lauren from IT. Thanks for joining, all."

Eddie led the meeting by reporting the usual progress against goals. Throughout the meeting, Eddie was his normal humorous self and by the end, Chris was starting to come out of his funk.

Eddie was thanking Raj and the IT folks again, and then he started laughing. "Before we break, I've got to tell you all a quick story about something we just did at KM. Last week, Sam sent us an e-mail telling us that they were in the process of setting up the 800 number for our customers to call if they have technical questions. He happened to mention in the e-mail that they were trying to come up with a name for the hotline; you know, something

STORY MATRIX - CHRIS

		Leadership Performance Skills				
		Culture/ Company	Motivation	Partnering	Clients	Me
Story Types	Success	Last Sand Dune Great Stuff	Digging deep Name that tune	Power Junk	Elevator pitch	Mother Pucker's
	Failure	Shake up	I've Been Moved	Myopic	Onion Rings	Long staircase
	Fun	Intramural "I'm new"	Rancor	Cowboys, big hats	Name That Hot Line	Bongle
	Legends	Organization Man				

FIGURE 9.1 Chris' Story Matrix

NAME THAT HOT LINE

Last week, Sam sent us an e-mail telling us that they were in the process of naming the 800 number for customers to call into if they have technical questions. So when we went in to meet with their team yesterday, before we started going through the details, we opened with a slide of the names that we had come up with for the line...just as a joke. We came up with names like "The 'You Really Expect Us To Help?' Line," "The 'For Assistance, Ask a Teenager' Line" "The 'Hold. Hope. Hold Some More' Line," and "The 'You Need Way More Help Than We Can Offer' Line." It was great! We had everyone rolling.

The Lessons:
Clients love having fun too
Listen for opportunities to have some fun

The Applications:
Build relationships
Motivate your team

I G N I T E

more creative than 'Technical Help Line.' So when we went in to meet with their team yesterday, before we started going through the details, we opened with a slide of the names that we had come up with for the line. Just as a joke, we came up with names like the 'You Really Expect Us to Help?' line, the 'For Assistance, Ask a Teenager' line, the 'Hold. Hope. Hold Some More' line, and the 'You Need Way More Help Than We Can Offer' line. It was great! We had everyone rolling."

Chris was laughing and starting to rally. "That's great, Eddie. I can just see you guys doing that. Make sure I get a copy of those names. That's one for the book!"

Kara and Rod walked into Chris's office at 9 AM sharp with an extra large, piping hot coffee.

Kara, handing Chris the coffee, said, "We come bearing gifts."

Chris was still chuckling over Eddie's story but he got immediately serious. "Ahhh. You read my mind. Thank you kindly. Sit down. Let's roll up our sleeves on this one."

Rod began, "Alright, Kara and I are trying to sort this out. We caught up with Jill, but only for a few minutes. She's joining us here. None of this is making any sense. We still can't figure out how Sam made the assumptions he did."

Jill, one of RJ's systems experts, walked into Chris's office and sat down, flipping through a stack of e-mails. Jill was all business. "Hey folks. I just printed all of the e-mail correspondence to and from our team and Sam's, and it's a mystery. Why the heck they made these design decisions is beyond me. But we need to reverse it all, and fast."

"Wait a sec," said Chris. "We can't just assume it's all their fault."

"Seems to be," responded Kara.

Jill agreed. "Yup."

"Guys, come on," said Chris. "What are we going to do, call Sam and say, 'Well, you sure made some bad decisions. Bet you feel stupid!'? That's not going to solve the problem. We are in deep here. If we miss this launch, that means marketing and sales have to mothball all of the effort and materials they've put together, and our IT group will reprioritize us to who knows when. We're talking major wasted dollars."

After a long discussion and brainstorming, Chris decided to get Sam on the phone and try to determine where they got off the rails.

"Just stay positive," Chris said as he dialed the phone. "I don't have to remind you that these people are important business partners to all of RJ." Sam answered. "Sam? Chris Olson from RJ. How are you?"

"Been better, Chris," Sam said, very matter-of-factly.

"I've got my core team here, Sam, and Eddie's on the line too. He's in our Chicago offices today."

Sam lightened up a bit. "Eddie, I heard you had a good meeting with my process group yesterday. They were still laughing about your hotline ideas this morning."

"That's good to hear," said Eddie, chuckling. "We had some fun with that. Anytime you need some rules badly broken, I'm your man."

Chris got back to business. "Sam, we are calling because we are concerned about your note this morning. You know how much we have riding on this launch. Frankly, you've scared the hell out of us. Can we talk about how this happened?"

Sam asked Chris to hold while he connected a couple of his folks to the call. Both teams spent a few minutes replaying the last couple of weeks of action, and several communications issues became clear as they talked.

Chris said, "I'm starting to see where we went wrong. It looks like we all made assumptions about what the other people were thinking all the way along. And once we got down the wrong path, those assumptions kept getting bigger and bigger."

"Yeah, I think that's right," said Sam, sounding defeated. "And here we are. I'm afraid that if we don't solve our communications problems, that we will just continue to grind and let each other down. Worse, we will cost each other a lot of money."

Chris remembered a story that he had written down after moving here two years ago to take this job. "We can fix this. I know we can. This team hasn't worked together very long. In fact, most of our team has literally moved here for this particular project. So we are still ironing out a lot of wrinkles. I don't know if you all know this, but I moved my family here two years ago for this job, and it was a mess. We went through all of the usual stuff: listing the house, finding a new one, moving the furniture (and the kids), and making sure the dog had a new vet. We did our homework on the new schools, met the neighbors, and started trying to fit into our new community. You've all been through this. It's pretty tough stuff, right? You feel like you are leaving everyone and everything behind. But when you stop and think about it, the infrastructure is the same. You still have a house to go home to. You've got your kids in school. You've got a washer and dryer, and the barbeque grill. You've got your office here at work and the computer and the café. So, all of the systems and stuff is the same. By all appearances, you've got everything you need. But it's not the same. None of the glue is there. The relationship you had with your dry cleaner is gone. And the guy in the office next to yours is someone you don't know. And you get lost on your way to the soccer field to pick up the kids. But your to-dos don't stop to wait for you to figure all of this out. They just keep coming. And you have to find time to figure all of this out while you are putting some glue between all of the people you need to work with. Folks, this is our challenge. We are coming together like we all just moved to a new place. We are trying to sort everything out, build relationships, and get the work done, but sometimes we get lost on the way."

"I think that's right." Sam was reflective. "That's well said, Chris. And like new neighbors, we need to go out of our way to help each other. We're just new at this. And you know what, my team is going through the same thing. The question is, How do we put this 'glue' between us quickly? Maybe it starts with stating our assumptions. I know we can do better at this and you all can too."

The two teams put together an "assumptions list" and some others tactics for how to question assumptions and enhance their communications, and Rod and Sam agreed to put together a plan for making the launch.

Wrapping up, Chris said, "Thanks, Sam. And thanks to your team. We can do this." Sam hung up, leaving Eddie on the line. "What do you think, team?"

Rod was looking uncertain. "Not sure what to think. I'm relieved. But I'm also realistic, Chris. I still don't see how we can pull this off."

"Honestly, I don't either," agreed Jill. "We have too few resources and not enough time."

"I hear you," Chris said, taking charge. "We are under the gun. Let me remind each of you in this room, and you too, Eddie, that you were all brought here to make this a success. Remember? And there was a reason for that. You are the best that RJ has. I'm not blowing sunshine here. You are, and you know it. Don't act like

STORY MATRIX - CHRIS

		Leadership Performance Skills			
		Culture/ Company	Motivation	Partnering	Clients	Me
Story Types	Success	Last Sand Dune Great Stuff	Digging deep Name that tune	Power drink	Elevator pitch	Mother Pucker's
	Failure	Shake-up	I've Been Moved	Myopic	Onion Rings	Long staircase
	Fun	Intramural "I'm over it"	Run...			
	Legends	Organization Man				

FIGURE 9.2 Chris' Story Matrix

I'VE BEEN MOVED

This team is still ironing out a lot of wrinkles. It's like moving to another city. You feel like you are leaving everyone and everything behind. But when you stop and think about it, you still have a house to go home to. You've got your office here at work and the computer and the café. So, all of the systems and stuff is the same. But it's not the same. None of the glue is there. The relationship you had with your dry cleaner is gone. And the guy in the office next to yours is someone you don't know. But your to-do's don't stop to wait for you to figure all of this out. And you have to find time to figure all of this out while you are putting some glue between all of the people you need to work with.

The Lessons:
Building strong teams takes time
Don't mistake infrastructure and appearances for trust

The Applications:
Build trust
Set context for difficult challenges

I   G   N   I   T   E

you've never been in this situation before! That's exactly why we chose you for this role. You've been through the desert before."

Sarcastically, Eddie said, "Uh-oh, here he goes."

Chris was getting fired up. "That's right, I am. Look, I'm here with you. Just put aside your business hats for a second and humor me. Imagine that we are on a journey through the desert. We got off track, and now our supplies are running low and we are tired and thirsty. We are walking up and down the huge sand dunes, with the sun beating down on us all day. At night we are nearly freezing. And all we see as we climb the next sand dune are more dunes—as far as the eye can see. It looks like it's impossible to survive. We don't have enough supplies to make it. Looking across the horizon at all of those dunes makes it seem like the only choice is to lay down and die. But we decide to keep going until we literally fall over. Days go by and we are barely still walking. Finally, we come to the top of a huge dune, and we see the ocean."

"He's crazy, but he's right," said Kara, looking at Jill and Rod. "We just need to keep putting one foot in front of the other. We are always resource-constrained. But with better handoffs, we can do this."

Chris added, "We *will* do this. I know it."

The team broke as Chris reminded them about the 3 PM meeting to discuss the launch strategy with the marketing folks.

Jill walked into the conference room at 3:05 PM. "Where is everyone? I thought we had the meeting with marketing!"

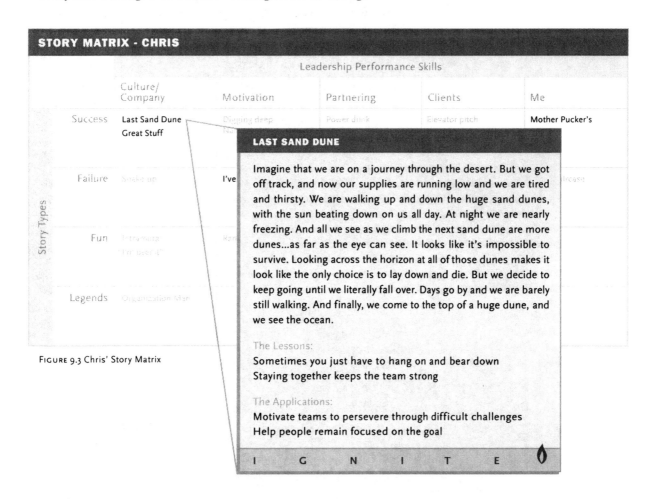

Figure 9.3 Chris' Story Matrix

Rod shrugged his shoulders. "I just checked e-mail. Nobody cancelled. I've got Eddie on the phone."

"Glad you could all be here," said Eddie, chiming in.

Jill was shaking her head. "I've got a bad feeling in my bones."

Just then, Chris walked into the conference room with Kara and three people from marketing and got straight to the point. "Another problem, folks. Tim here got a call from our advertising firm, and somehow they got the launch date wrong. Our campaign went live today, and they've got the launch date a week earlier than planned."

Eddie said, "Excuse me while I open this window on the 55th floor."

Rod was shaking his head. "How the..."

"Rod, I don't know," interrupted Tim, one of RJ's key marketing people. He was clearly frustrated. "You can bet I'm going to find out. But the damage is done. I'm sorry. Unless you've got a time machine, the cat's out of the bag. Can't put it back in."

"Suddenly, it feels like midnight. I'm tired," said Rod.

Chris's team asked the marketing team a bunch of questions and they discussed possible solutions, but there were none to be had. The marketing team moved on to another meeting, leaving Chris's team sitting in the conference room with Eddie on the phone.

"We seem to be going backwards today," Chris offered. "First the KM glitch, and now this."

Jill stepped in. "Well, the first thing we need to do is let Sam and the KM team know the bad news. But before we do that, we need to revise our plan. I think it's clear to all of us that accelerating this plan means really moving some big priorities around. That's not going to be easy, but it can be done. And, we are going to have to convince Sam to do the same thing."

The team sketched out a revised launch plan that involved bringing in additional resources and reconfiguring most of their activities for next month. Through the discussion, it became clear that they were all going to be working long hours to pull it off.

"Rod, did you say midnight?" said Eddie. "It feels more like 4 AM."

"I know this means long hours, but we can do it, guys," said Jill.

Chris was lost in space but looking at Jill. "Jill, tell that story you told me the other day."

"Which one?" asked Jill, surprised.

"The one about your hockey game. That is a great story, and we could use that one right now."

Jill smiled. "Oh yeah. Sure. Guys, as some of you know, I play women's hockey on a very amateur team called the Mother Pucker's." Eddie burst out laughing and was joined by the rest of the group. "My team is an eclectic mix of good athletes, moms, older women, and some young ones—with some aggression issues. We got invited to a tournament in Minneapolis a few weekends ago and so, just for fun, we went. Of course, we figured we would get pummeled by the women up there. These girls grow up with hockey sticks in their cribs and we are just a bunch of posers. We played three games, and much to our shock, we won the first game against a better team! I was so excited, I felt like I was ten years old. What's so cool about hockey is how complex it is. I'm still learning the game, but some things really came together that weekend. We were late in that first game and everyone was really tired. You're trying so hard to make a play and make a difference that sometimes you forget that what you really need is help. Hockey moves and changes so fast that it makes perfect sense to get off the ice as soon as you start to feel tired. Because the game doesn't stop for subs—like football and other sports—fresh players are always coming in and out. With about a minute left, I went to the bench, and one of my teammates just had fire in her eyes as she went in for me. She went in and just outskated everybody on the ice. She ended up scoring the winning goal with 28 seconds left. It was amazing. It was almost like I knew she was going to win it before it happened. But in talking about it with my team after the game, it became clear that the other team had left their best players on the ice. And they were just too tired to stop her. If they had subbed, they would have probably beaten us. But they didn't. And we ended taking the bronze in the tournament."

"That is a great story! I didn't know you played hockey. That's so cool," said Rod, smiling and pumping his fist. "Wait until my daughter hears about this!"

Kara was thinking. "I've never thought about hockey that way. As a matter of fact, I've never thought about hockey!" Everyone laughed as she continued. "But what you say is true, Jill. You have to realize when you need help and you have to ask for it."

Eddie was still laughing. "I can't get over the name—Mother Pucker's. I love that!"

STORY MATRIX - CHRIS

Leadership Performance Skills

		Culture/ Company	Motivation	Partnering	Clients	Me
Story Types	Success	Last Sand Dune Great Stuff	Digging deep Name that Tune	Power duck	Elevator pitch	Mother Pucker's
	Failure	Shake-up	I've			
	Fun	Intramural "I'm over it"				
	Legends	Organization Man				

FIGURE 9.4 Chris' Story Matrix

MOTHER PUCKER'S

A colleague of mine told me this story: I play women's hockey on a very amateur team called the Mother Pucker's. What's so cool about hockey is how complex it is. I'm still learning the game, but some things really came together recently. We were late in a game and everyone was really tired. You're trying so hard to make a play and make a difference that sometimes you forget that what you really need is help. Hockey moves and changes so fast that it makes perfect sense to get off the ice as soon as you start to feel tired. With about a minute left, I went to the bench, and one of my teammates just had fire in her eyes as she went in for me. She went in and just out-skated everybody on the ice. She ended up scoring the winning goal with 28 seconds left.

The Lessons:
Everyone needs help
Don't try to do everything by yourself
People appreciate being asked to help

The Applications:
Acknowledge how hard people are working
Demonstrate that it's okay for people to ask for help
Prevent burnout

I   G   N   I   T   E

Jill said, "Well, I can't take credit for the name, but it is clever. It's a great group. But seriously, we just have to remember that when we're tired, we've got to help each other."

Eddie added, "That, and if you ever walk in missing a couple of front teeth, we'll know why!"

Chris was suddenly reflective. "I've said it before and I'll say it again; this team is the best. I learn something from you four every day, and I'm thankful for that. I seriously am. By the way, can we all huddle in my office later today? Is 6 PM too late?"

Late in the afternoon, Chris was meeting with the operations team that would be handling the inbound customer calls post-launch. They had been busy setting up the systems and they were now turning their attention to training associates on how to handle the customers. Chris had been asked to describe the offering in detail and help the operations team design an approach that would delight customers.

Chris looked at Jack, the head of operations, but addressed his whole team of 25. "All of your questions have been dead on. My team and I really appreciate the support you are giving us on this launch. I realize that this KM partnership throws some wrinkles at you all, because there are some handoffs that you don't normally have to make."

"This is true," said Jack. "I'm sure my folks can handle it, but we will just need to be very clear with the customer about what we can and can't do."

Chris nodded. "You're right, Jack. I know your team will handle it. I must admit to all of you that I do worry that we make the right trade-off between letting the customer know what we can and can't do and being flexible. We don't want to send people away unhappy."

Jack was a bit wary. "Chris, help us understand what that means."

"Well, it's not perfectly clear," said Chris, deciding to tell a story that he had thought he might need in this meeting. "Because we haven't launched yet, we won't know until we know. It's hard to predict what customers are going to ask for, and you all know better than me that we can't plan for everything. But I'd like to try to illustrate what I'm getting at with a story. I remember five or six years ago, I was working with a client's senior team as they were trying to prepare for another big launch like this. We had gathered to discuss what kind of service we could provide in support of a new product. These senior folks, predictably, wanted to offer premier customer service. So, in order to get the juices flowing on what premier service looked like, I had each person go around the room and tell a story of a great customer service experience. Then, I had every leader tell a story about when they had had rotten service. That's when the flood gates opened! One of the senior-most people in the room, a guy named Austin, told this story, and I'll tell it to you just as he told it to us."

"Austin said, 'I was traveling with my team, and we stopped for dinner. We picked a place that was definitely not going to win any awards, but it was fine. You know, the type of place with pictures of the food on the menu. But it was a decent place and I thought it would be a good place to talk. We sat down, and when the waiter approached to take our order, here's what happened:

> *Austin:* I see from the picture here that you have onion rings on top of the meatloaf. I don't want the meatloaf, but I would love to have a side order of onion rings.
> *Waiter:* We don't have onion rings.
> Austin: Oh, I see them on the meatloaf and I just assumed you had them.
> *Waiter:* Well, we do, but they only come with the meatloaf.
> *Austin:* I see. But I just want a side order of them.
> Waiter: I told you, they come with the meatloaf. We don't serve side orders.
> *Austin, getting frustrated:* Fine. I'll have an order of the meatloaf—hold the meatloaf.
> *Waiter, not amused:* Sir, we can't do that.
> *Austin, getting angry:* You know what, why don't you get your manager out here for me, okay?

At this point, the waiter left to get the manager and I thought that this problem would be quickly solved.

> *Manager:* Sir, may I help you?
> *Austin, chuckling:* I think we just have a misunderstanding. No big deal. Do you guys have onion rings?
> *Manager:* Yes we do.
> *Austin:* Great. See, I'd like to have some onion rings, and I see from the picture on the menu that you have them. But I don't want the meatloaf. I simply want a side order of onion rings.
> *Manager:* I'm sorry sir, we don't serve them separately.

Chris was shaking his head. "My client never did get his onion rings. And as he told this story, his face got redder and redder, to the point that he was almost shouting. All of the other leaders were laughing and nodding, because they had heard the story so many times and they loved it. The story was a perfect illustration of what can happen when a company doesn't understand how to help its employees provide great customer service."

"That's great!" said Jack, laughing along with all of his people. "I can just see that happening!"

"Ah, but the story doesn't end there," said Chris. "I happened to have brought along one of my new people to watch the session—sort of a training exercise. Because it was midmorning at that point, I wrote him a quick note, wrapped the note around my mobile phone, and handed it to him. The note said:

20 orders of onion rings for lunch today. Please make this happen.
Thanks Josh.

So Josh quietly disappeared from the back of the room and I turned the discussion to examples of positive customer service. At noon, I was reviewing what we had discussed in the morning session and previewing the afternoon session. The leaders were ready for lunch. Just in time, Josh came in the back of the room with two people carrying two trays of 20 little white Styrofoam containers. I asked them to come to the front of the room. The leaders wondered what the heck I was doing. I said to the leader who had told the restaurant story, 'Austin, what are we having for lunch?' Austin said 'Huh?' So I asked again, 'What are we having for lunch?' He was getting quickly frustrated with me. 'Chris, how should I know?' he said. I replied, 'Think about it.' Austin was now mad. 'Chris, I don't know. What are you getting at?' With great ceremony, I opened one of the containers. 'We're having onion rings, Austin. Just like you like them.' At that point, everyone in the room erupted in laughter and we settled down to feast on onion rings. For this client, the story became an illustration of how we could encourage the company's substantial customer service force not to let inflexible systems and processes get in the way of service and to look for opportunities to delight clients and go above and beyond."

Jack was staring at Chris. "That is great, man. It reminds me of a couple of restaurant experiences I've had! It does illustrate the trade-off between flexibility and rules. And that's always one of our biggest challenges." Jack and his team took some time to discuss how and where it would be appropriate to bend the rules to accommodate clients and where it wouldn't, and as that wrapped up, Chris thanked them and headed back to his office for his last meeting of the day.

Chris looked up as Jill and Rod walk into his office. "Hey, you two. Thanks for joining me. This is going to be quick. Let's get Eddie on the phone." Chris punched in Eddie as Kara walked into his office. "Eddie? Hey, thanks for doing this. I'm sure you've got a million things going on over there."

Eddie asked, "Am I in trouble again?"

"I know you all want to get home, so I'll make this quick," Chris said, ignoring Eddie's antics.

"You know how you always kid me for keeping my 'Great Stuff' file?"

"The one where you seem to keep everything that's ever been said about each of us?" Jill asked. "We just figured you actually work for the FBI."

STORY MATRIX - CHRIS

		Leadership Performance Skills				
		Culture/ Company	Motivation	Partnering	Clients	Me
Story Types	Success	Last Sand Dune Great Stuff	Digging deep Name that tune	Power dunk	Elevator pitch	Mother Pucker's
	Failure	Shake up	I've Been Moved	Myopic	Onion Rings	Long staircase
	Fun	Intramural "I'm over it"				
	Legends	Organization Man				

FIGURE 9.5 Chris' Story Matrix

ONION RINGS

A client saw onion rings in a picture on the menu of a not-so-great restaurant. When he asked for an order, the waiter told him they didn't serve onion rings. My client asked about the picture and was told "the onion rings just come on the meatloaf." The client asked for the manager, thinking that he would straighten out the situation. When he asked the manager whether they had onion rings, the manager said "Yes sir." So my client told the manager he didn't want the meatloaf, just the rings. The manager said "Sorry sir, we don't serve them that way."

The Lessons:
Don't blindly follow the rules
Help people understand ways they can accommodate customers
Be flexible within reason

The Applications:
Demonstrate the gray areas of customer service
Build understanding of different levels of customer service
Teach people to be flexible but smart

I   G   N   I   T   E

Chris laughed. "See what I mean? I'll never live this down! No, all of the stuff I keep is *great stuff*, remember? Not the bad stuff. And the FBI doesn't have to know about *that* stuff."

Eddie, pretending to get choked up, said, "We just figured that you keep that file because you...miss us...so much...when we're away."

"No," Chris said, "but strangely enough, Eddie's come close to the truth." Jill, Kara, and Rod all laughed at that thought as Eddie burst into a mock meltdown. "You all know why I keep it. Because I want to remind us all of why this team works so well," Chris said, dramatically pulling a printed e-mail out of a file folder. "For instance, remember this one? Here's an e-mail from Rod to me about Kara last March. It says:

Chris—
Just a quick note to say that Kara just made my day. You've gotta know, because I know she won't say anything to you, that she is the best I've ever seen at working with our software team. She seems to have earned so much credibility with them so fast that they will do anything for her. I am so glad that you got her to join this team. She makes us all smarter and better, and that makes my life so much easier and more fun. Please tell her I appreciate it.
Rod.

Chris paused to look at everyone. "Remember that one? I do."

Rod was chuckling and nodding his head. "I needed to remember that this morning!"

"I wasn't that person this morning," Kara chimed in. "That's why you didn't remember."

Chris moved on. "Or how about this one? This one's from last May, when we were going through that systems migration. Jill wrote:

Chris—
Eddie rocks. That's right. He does. I just walked out of a meeting where it looked like the world was coming apart because of this migration. Everyone was pointing fingers and getting upset and Eddie, as usual, just broke in with some hilarious (and sick) comments that not only lightened the mood but made it immediately clear that we were just spinning our wheels. I swear, Eddie made the meeting go from bloodbath to laugh track in about two nanoseconds. Where did we find this guy?

Eddie jumped on that, "At the Home for Failed Comedians?"

Jill was laughing as she remembered that meeting. "Ha! Eddie, you were killing us! You had everyone rolling about how customers would react when the system didn't work, and the questions they would call in with. You were doing their voices and everything. You were on a roll!"

Chris added, "Yes, we've certainly all been victimized by Eddie! Here's another one. I wrote this down after Kara and Eddie had coffee with me one day and they were telling me about how Jill went above and beyond the day before that presentation we had about budgeting. They said, and I quote:

> We discovered at about 7 PM that the assumptions we had made for license fees were way low. All of us just sort of looked at each other, knowing that the numbers we had prepared were now complete nonsense. It was going to take hours to figure out the right numbers, redo all of the projections, run the spreadsheets, rewrite the presentation, and copy and bind it. We were in for a long night. Then Jill looks at us and says, 'Kara, you've got your daughter's dance recital in 30 minutes. You are not staying. And Eddie, you just told me 20 minutes ago that Paul is expecting you at dinner across town. Go, both of you. I can handle this. Most of it is just busywork and we will just stumble over each other.

"Thanks, you guys," Jill said. "I do remember that. I think that was the first time I had pulled an all-nighter since college. And, as I recall, you three brought me a four-gallon cup of coffee and a box of chocolate after that meeting!"

Chris, looking directly at Rod, said, "And last but not least, I have an e-mail about Rod. From Jim at KM, no less."

Eddie yelled "Ahhhh! The client from hell!"

"Formerly from hell, thanks to Rod," Chris amended. "Remember how Jim got so hot under the collar when he thought we had locked his people out of the system? And then Rod figured out that our IT folks had accidentally disabled their access? Rod not only talked Jim down from the ledge, but he also made it clear to Jim, ever-so-diplomatically, that Jim couldn't say the things he had said to our team and get away with it. Here's Jim's note:

Chris—

Just wanted to tell that I talked with Rod about what happened. It looks like it was a misunderstanding. You should know that I appreciated Rod getting right on the problem and solving it quickly. He is a talented guy, and my team really likes him. Rod also helped us understand how we need to communicate with the IT folks. He made himself very clear and he let us know how much he values our business.

Thanks, Jim.

"Oh, must have been painful for Stiff Jim to write that one!" said Eddie. "None of us would say that about Rod!" he said, laughing. "You know I'm kidding, bud! I've always said you should run for high office!"

FIGURE 9.6 Chris' Story Matrix

Chris added, "No doubt about that! Rod, I'll be your campaign manager." Chris looked around the room. "This is the good stuff, folks. After a day like today, I felt the need to remind you all how great you are by telling your stories. You are all a gift to me and to this organization. It's a pleasure to work with you, and it's a pleasure to be a part of creating these stories together."

"So, I'm *not* in trouble?" said Eddie.

THE END OF THIS STORY

If you spent one whole day doing nothing but looking for stories that inspire, you would find enough from your own life and the lives of those around you to fill a Win Book and Story Matrix. You could then turn to actually telling these stories, and giving yourself and those around you a tremendous gift. I encourage you to do it.

Telling stories gets results—for your leadership, for your organization, for your life. And these results that you get from telling stories— stronger connections, better performance—are a "destination" of sorts. But remember, the journey is as important as the destination.

Think for a moment of all the things that inspire you: the birth of a beautiful baby; the unvarnished joy of children; an elderly person's smile; your favorite song; an unexpected gift from a friend; the power and beauty of nature; the thrill of a come-from-behind victory; bare knuckled, all-out effort. All of these things connect to the emotions—love, fear, awe—that make life so rich. These are the journeys of heroes. And these heroes and their stories *are all around you.* All you need to do is be open to them. Absorb them. Tell them. Be a hero. What's your story?

CHAPTER 9:
SUMMARY

THE BITS AND BULLETS

- Stories that motivate and inspire don't have to be the stuff of legend.

- Leaders who are authentic are the ones who inspire people.

- Stories that motivate and inspire connect to our core values—what we care about deeply.

- Don't avoid the emotional component of stories, because engaging emotions is what truly inspires.

- In choosing a motivational and inspirational story, be sure the story can positively answer at least one of these questions:
  - Does the story help people bond together?
  - Does the story create a path to possibility?
  - Does the story allow for some fun?

- Absorb the stories that are all around you.

THE PICTURES

Chris's Story Matrix with the **Name That Hot Line** Story in Detail

Chris's Story Matrix with the **I've Been Moved** Story in Detail

Chris's Story Matrix with the **Last Sand Dune** Story in Detail

Chris's Story Matrix with the **Mother Pucker's** Story in Detail

Chris's Story Matrix with the **Onion Rings** Story in Detail

Chris's Story Matrix with the **Great Stuff** Story in Detail

THE STORIES

Name That Hot Line
Look for opportunities to inject some humor in an otherwise mundane request

I've Been Moved
Working in teams can feel like moving to a new city—everything looks the same, but there is none of the "glue" that holds it all together

Last Sand Dune
Sometimes success is made up of just continuing to bear down and put one foot in front of the other

Mother Pucker's
Knowing yourself well enough to know when you are too tired to contribute and then asking for help is critical

Onion Rings
Otherwise mundane stories can be the stuff of legend that motivates and inspires people to perform

Great Stuff
Capturing and telling stories and anecdotes about your people serves to remind them of their key strengths and inspires them to perform even better

CHAPTER 9:
MY THOUGHTS AND IDEAS

APPENDIX

PICTURES

NOTES

INTRODUCTION

1. Richard Saul Wurman, *Information Anxiety 2* (Indianapolis: Que, 2001), 79.

2. Dan Pink, *A Whole New Mind* (New York: Penguin, 2005), 50.

PART ONE: PROBLEM

CHAPTER 1

1. Edna St. Vincent Millay, *Huntsman, What Quarry?*

2. Linda Tischler, "The Beauty of Simplicity," *Fast Company* (November 2005): 52–54.

3. Thomas Davenport, *Thinking for a Living* (Boston: Harvard Business School Press, 2005), 122.

4. Ibid., 123.

5. Ibid., 125.

6. Taylor Hess, conversation in Bloomington, Indiana, 5 November 2005.

7. Joel Achenbach, "The Too-Much-Information Age," *Washington Post* (12 March 1999): A01.

8. Clive Thompson, "Meet the Life Hackers," *New York Times* (16 October 2005): 40–45.

9. Ibid.

10. Ibid.

11. Nathan Shedroff, quoted in Richard Saul Wurman's book, *Information Anxiety 2*, 28.

12. John Schwartz, "The Level of Discourse Continues to Slide," *New York Times* (28 September 2003).

13. Thompson, "Meet the Life Hackers," 40–45.

14. Eric Chester, conversation with author in San Diego, California, 21 June 2005.

15. Ted Koppel, interview with Scott Simon on National Public Radio's *Weekend Edition*, 12 November 2005.

16. Kasey Diulus, conversation in Chicago, Illinois, 24 October 2005.

17. Annette Simmons, *The Story Factor* (Cambridge: Perseus Publishing, 2001), 51.

18. Schwartz, "The Level of Discourse Continues to Slide."

19. David Carr, "Taken to a New Place, by a TV in the Palm," *New York Times* (18 December 2005).

20. Neil Postman, in a speech given to the German Informatics Society, Stuttgart, Germany, 11 October 1990.

21. Wurman, *Information Anxiety 2*, i.

22. Martin Siegel, "Falling Asleep At Your Keyboard: The Case for Computer Imagination," academic paper, 2003, 1–6.

23. Paul Cole, quoted in "Fast Talk: The State of the Customer Economy," *Fast Company* (September 2001): 80.

24. Martin Siegel, conversation in Bloomington, Indiana, 2002.

25. Peter Drucker, "The Next Information Revolution," *Forbes ASAP* (24 August 1998): 47.

PART TWO: SOLUTION

CHAPTER 2

1. Simmons, *The Story Factor*, 54.

2. Robert McKee, "Storytelling That Moves People," *Harvard Business Review* (June 2003): 51–55.

3. Ibid.

4. Edward Tufte, "Power Corrupts. PowerPoint Corrupts Absolutely," *Wired* (September 2003), 118.

5. Edward Tufte, "The Cognitive Styles of PowerPoint" (academic paper, May 2003), 4.

6. Howard Gardner, *Leading Minds: An Anatomy of Leadership* (New York: HarperCollins, 1995), 62.

7. Doris Lessing, as quoted by Robert Fulford, *The Triumph of Narrative. The Massey Lecture* (Toronto: Canadian Broadcasting Company, 1999): Tape 4-A.

8. Robert McKee, *Story* (New York: HarperCollins, 1997), 111.

9. Seth Godin, *All Marketers Are Liars* (New York: Penguin, 2005,) 2.

10. Thomas Davenport, *Thinking for a Living* (Boston: Harvard Business School Press, 2003), 111.

11. David Snowden, "The Paradox of Story," *The Journal of Straggly & Scenario Planning* (November 1999): 1–8.

12. Fulford, *The Triumph of Narrative*, Tape 1-A.

13. Benjamin Franklin, as quoted in Richard Saul Wurman's book, *Information Anxiety 2*, 77.

14. Simmons, *The Story Factor*, 5.

15. Tom Atkinson and Jocelyn Davis, "Principles of Workplace Learning" (Forum Corporation, 2004): 25.

16. Simmons, *The Story Factor*, 54.

17. Sam Wineburg, *Historical Thinking and Other Unnatural Acts* (Philadelphia: Temple University Press, 2001), 21.

18. Scott Carbonara, conversation in Chicago, Illinois, 2006.

19. Simmons, *The Story Factor*, 51.

20. Roger Schank, *Tell Me a Story: Narrative and Intelligence* (Evanston: Northwestern University Press, 1998), 115.

21. Neil Postman, "Science and the Story," *First Things* 69 (January 1997): 29–32.

22. Ray Angeli, conversation in Chicago, Illinois, 2006.

23. Simmons, *The Story Factor*, 34.

24. Malcolm Gladwell, *The Tipping Point* (New York: Little, Brown and Company, 2000), 171.

CHAPTER 3

1. Dan Pink, author of *A Whole New Mind*, podcast interview with Elliott Masie, 10 August 2005.

2. Del Jones, "The Indian Art of Storytelling Seeps into the Boardroom," *USA TODAY*, (19 September 2004): 2.

3. Simmons, *The Story Factor*, 19.

4. Tom Peters, *Leadership* (London: Dorling Kindersley, 2005), 80.

5. Gladwell, *The Tipping Point*, 183.

6. Ibid., 177.

7. Ibid., 174.

8. Ibid., 186.

9. John Kotter and Dan Cohen, *Heart of Change* (Boston: Harvard Business School Press, 2002), 80.

10. Gladwell, *The Tipping Point*, 184.

11. Jim Shaffer, "Best Practices in Employee Communication," Right Management Consultants report (2004): 27.

12. Ibid., 29.

13. Ibid., 27.

14. Ibid., 29.

15. John Egan, quoted in "Best Practices in Employee Communication," 37.

16. John Seely Brown, *Storytelling in Organizations* (Burlington: Elsevier Butterworth-Heinemann, 2005), 82.

17. John Seely Brown and Paul Duguid, *The Social Life of Information* (Boston: Harvard Business School Press, 2000), 135.

PART THREE: TOOLS

CHAPTER 4

1. Tim Sanders, "Love is the Killer App," *Fast Company* (February 2002): 64.

2. Richard Stone, quoted in Thomas Stewart's article, "The Cunning Plots of Leadership," 2.

3. Dan Pink, *A Whole New Mind*, 1.

4. McKee, *Story*, 73.

5. Philip Evans and Thomas Wurster, *Blown to Bits* (Boston: Harvard Business School Press, 2000), 15.

6. Gunnar Nilsson, conversation in Highland Park, Illinois, 2003.

7. Simmons, *The Story Factor*, 233.

8. Plato's *Meno*, as found in *The Collected Dialogues of Plato* (Princeton: Princeton University Press, 1961), 364.

CHAPTER 5

1. Simmons, *The Story Factor*, 195.

2. Stephen Denning, "Telling Tales," *Harvard Business Review* (May 2004): 122–129.

3. Charlotte Linde, quoted in Thomas Stewart's article, "The Cunning Plots of Leadership," 1.

4. Rosamund Stone Zander and Benjamin Zander, *The Art of Possibility* (New York: Penguin, 2000), 12.

5. Simmons, *The Story Factor*, 29.

6. Herb Kelleher, "A Culture of Commitment," *Leader to Leader* No. 4 (1997): 20–24.

7. Jim Collins, *Good To Great* (New York: HarperCollins, 2001), 87.

8. Ibid., 87.

9. Raymond Chandler, *Raymond Chandler Speaking* (Berkeley and Los Angeles, Calif.: University of California Press, 1997).

10. Simmons, *The Story Factor*, 41.

11. Simmons, *The Story Factor*, 10.

12. Peters, *Leadership*, 80.

CHAPTER 6

1. Godin, *All Marketers Are Liars*, 1.

2. Larry Bossidy and Ram Charan, *Execution* (New York: Random House, 2002), 89.

3. Godin, *All Marketers Are Liars*, 171.

4. Iain Mackenzie, conversation in Singapore, 11 October 2005.

5. Harlynne Geisler, *Storytelling Professionally* (Engelwood: Libraries Unlimited, 1997), 7.

6. Russ Roberts, conversation in Winnetka, Illinois, 2002.

7. Martin Siegel, conversation in Bloomington, Indiana, 2003.

8. Simmons, *The Story Factor*, 151.

9. John Steiner, "Use of Stories in Clinical Research and Health Policy," *Journal of the American Medical Association* (14 December 2005): 2901–2904.

10. Wikipedia, http://en.wikipedia.org/wiki/storytelling.

11. David Holt and Bill Mooney, *The Storyteller's Guide* (Little Rock: August House, 1996), 9.

12. Charna Halpern, Del Close, and Kim Johnson, *Truth in Comedy: The Manual of Improvisation* (Colorado Springs: Meriwether Publishing Ltd., 1993), 46.

13. Simmons, *The Story Factor*, 41.

14. McKee, "Storytelling That Moves People."

15. McKee, *Story*, 113.

16. Simmons, *The Story Factor*, 229.

17. Brown and Duguid, *The Social Life of Information*, 107.

18. Simmons, *The Story Factor*, 213.

19. Eckhart Tolle, *The Power of Now* (Novato: New World Library, 1999), 85.

20. Tihamer von Ghyczy, "The Fruitful Flaws of Strategy Metaphors," *Harvard Business Review* (September 2003): 86–95.

PART FOUR: TECHNIQUES

CHAPTER 7

1. Stephen Denning, quoted in Lucy Kellaway's article, "Once Upon a Time, We Had Managers—Not Storytellers," *The Financial Times* (10 May 2004): 10.

2. Simmons, *The Story Factor*, 19.

3. Thomas Stewart, quoting Howard Gardner in "The Cunning Plots of Leadership," 1.

4. Thomas Stewart, "The Cunning Plots of Leadership," *Fortune* (7 September 1998): 1.

5. Snowden, "The Paradox of Story."

CHAPTER 8

1. Richard Saul Wurman, *Information Anxiety 2*, 135.

2. Louis Gerstner, Jr., *Who Says Elephants Can't Dance? Inside IBM's Historic Turnaround* (New York: HarperCollins, 2002): p 43.

3. Godin, *All Marketers Are Liars*, 29.

4. Ibid., 8.

5. Rekha Balu, "Whirlpool Gets Real with Customers," *Fast Company* (December 1999): 1–2.

6. Natalie Goldberg, *Writing Down The Bones* (Boston: Shambhala, 1986), 53.

7. Godin, *All Marketers Are Liars*, 115.

8. Simmons, *The Story Factor*, 108.

CHAPTER 9

1. Stephen Denning, quoted in Lucy Kellaway's article, "Once Upon a Time, We Had Managers—Not Storytellers," 2.

2. Marcus Buckingham, "What Great Managers Do," *Harvard Business Review* (March 2005): 70–79.

3. Holt and Mooney, *The Storyteller's Guide,* 9.

4. McKee, "Storytelling That Moves People."

5. Denning, "Telling Tales."

6. McKee, "Storytelling That Moves People."

7. Holt and Mooney, *The Storyteller's Guide,* 8.

BIBLIOGRAPHY

Anthony, Mitch, and Scott West. *Storyselling for Financial Advisors*. Chicago: Kaplan, 2000.

Beck, John, and Thomas Davenport. *The Attention Economy*. Boston: Harvard Business School Press, 2001.

Bennis, Warren. *On Becoming a Leader*. Cambridge: Perseus, 1989.

Block, Peter. *Flawless Consulting*. San Francisco: Wiley, 1981.

Bossidy, Larry, and Ram Charan. *Execution*. New York: Random House, 2002.

Buckingham, Marcus, and Curt Coffman. *First, Break All the Rules*. New York: Simon & Schuster, 1999.

Bulfinch, Thomas. *Bulfinch's Mythology*. New York: Random House, 1998.

Burke, James. *The Pinball Effect*. Boston: Little, Brown & Company, 1996.

Byrne, David. *Envisioning Emotional Epistemological Information*. Germany: Steidl, 2003.

Campbell, Joseph. *The Hero with a Thousand Faces*. Princeton: Princeton University Press, 1949.

Campbell, Joseph. *The Power of Myth*. New York: Random House, 1988.

Charan, Ram, Stephen Drotter, and James Noel. *The Leadership Pipeline*. San Francisco: Wiley, 2001.

Cialdini, Robert. *Influence: The Psychology of Persuasion*. New York: William Morrow, 1984.

Coles, Robert. *The Call of Stories*. Boston: Houghton Mifflin, 1989.

Collins, James. *Good to Great*. New York: HarperCollins, 2001.

Collins, James, and Jerry Porras. *Built To Last,* New York: HarperCollins, 1994.

Covey, Stephen. *The 7 Habits of Highly Effective People*. New York: Simon & Schuster, 1989.

Csikszentmihalyi, Mihaly. *Flow*. New York: HarperCollins, 1990.

Davenport, Thomas. *Thinking for a Living*. Boston: Harvard Business School Press, 2005.

Denning, Steve. *The Springboard*. Boston: Butterworth-Heinemann, 2001.

Denning, Steve. *Squirrel Inc*. San Francisco: Jossey-Bass, 2004.

Dorner, Dietrich. *The Logic of Failure*. Cambridge: Perseus, 1996.

Drucker, Peter. *Managing for the Future*. New York: Penguin, 1992.

Estes, Clarissa Pinkola. *The Gift of Story*. New York: Ballantine Books, 1993.

Evans, Philip, and Thomas Wurster. *Blown to Bits*. Boston: Harvard Business School Press, 2000.

Farber, Steve. *The Radical Leap*. Chicago: Kaplan, 2004.

Fulford, Robert. *The Triumph of Narrative. The Massey Lecture*. Toronto: Canadian Broadcasting Company, 1999.

Gardner, Howard. *Leading Minds*. New York: HarperCollins, 1995.

Garvin, David. *Learning in Action*. Boston: Harvard Business School Press, 2000.

Geisler, Harlynne. *Storytelling Professionally*. Engelwood: Libraries Unlimited, 1997.

Gibson, William. *Pattern Recognition*. New York: Penguin, 2003.

Gitomer, Jeffrey. *Customer Satisfaction Is Worthless. Customer Loyalty Is Priceless*. Austin: Bard Press, 1998.

Gladwell, Malcolm. *Blink*. New York: Little, Brown and Company, 2005.

Gladwell, Malcolm. *The Tipping Point*. New York: Little, Brown and Company, 2000.

Gleick, James. *Faster*. New York: Random House, 1999.

Godin, Seth. *All Marketers Are Liars*. New York: Penguin, 2005.

Godin, Seth. *Purple Cow*. New York: Penguin, 2003.

Goldberg, Natalie. *Writing Down the Bones*. Boston: Shambhala, 1986.

Goldsmith, Marshall, Beverly Kaye, and Ken Shelton. *Learning Journeys*. Palo Alto: Davies-Black Publishing, 2000.

Goleman, Daniel, Richard Boyatzis, and Annie McKee. *Primal Leadership*. Boston: Harvard Business School Press, 2002.

Halpern, Charna, Del Close, and Kim Johnson. *Truth in Comedy*. Colorado Springs: Meriwether, 1993.

Hill, Linda. *Becoming A Manager*. Boston: Harvard Business School Press, 2003.

Hill, Sam. *60 Trends in 60 Minutes*. Hoboken: Wiley, 2002.

Holt, David, and Bill Mooney. *The Storyteller's Guide*. Little Rock: August House, 1996.

Jensen, Bill. *Simplicity*. Cambridge: Perseus, 2000.

Kotter, John. *Leading Change*. Boston: Harvard Business School Press, 1996.

Kotter, John, and Dan Cohen. *The Heart of Change*. Boston: Harvard Business School Press, 2002.

Kouzes, James, and Barry Pozner. *The Leadership Challenge*. San Francisco: Wiley, 2002.

Kouzes, James, and Barry Pozner. *The Leadership Challenge Planner*. San Francisco: Wiley, 1999.

Lakoff, George, and Mark Johnson. *Metaphors We Live By*. Chicago: University of Chicago Press, 1980.

Lewis, Michael. *Next*. New York: W.W. Norton & Company, 2001.

Lipman, Doug. *Improving Your Storytelling*. Little Rock: August House, 1999.

Losey, Mike, Sue Meisinger, and Dave Ulrich. *The Future of Human Resource Management*. Alexandria: Wiley & Sons, 2005.

MacDonald, Margaret Read. *The Storyteller's Start-up Book*. Little Rock: August House, 1993.

McKee, Robert. *Story*. New York: HarperCollins, 1997.

Moore, Geoffery A. *Crossing the Chasm*. New York: HarperCollins, 1991.

Nilsson, Gunnar. *Human Bandwidth*. Rapid City: Rapid Creek Publishing, 2002.

Patterson, Kerry, Joseph Grenny, Ron McMillan, and Al Switzler. *Crucial Conversations* New York: McGraw-Hill, 2002.

Peters, Tom. *Leadership*. London: Dorling Kindersley, 2005.

Peters, Tom. *The Brand You 50*. New York: Alfred A. Knopf, 1999.

Pink, Daniel. *A Whole New Mind*. New York: Penguin, 2005.

Porter, Michael. *Competitive Strategy*. New York: Free Press, 1980.

Postman, Neil. *Amusing Ourselves to Death*. New York: Penguin, 1985.

Putnam, Robert. *Bowling Alone*. New York: Simon & Schuster, 2000.

Rackham, Neil. *Spin Selling*. New York: McGraw-Hill, 1988.

Reichheld, Frederick. *The Loyalty Effect*. Boston: Harvard Business School Press, 1996.

Restak, Richard. *Mozart's Brain and the Fighter Pilot*. New York: Three Rivers Press, 2001.

Robinson, Dana Gaines, and James C. Robinson. *Performance Consulting*. San Francisco: Berrett-Koehler Publishers, 1995.

Rosenbach, William, and Robert Taylor, eds. *Contemporary Issues in Leadership*. Boulder: Westview Press, 1993.

Sanders, Tim. *Love Is the Killer App*. New York: Random House, 2002.

Schank, Roger. *Tell Me a Story: Narrative and Intelligence*. Evanston: Northwestern University Press, 1998.

Seely Brown, John, and Paul Duguid. *The Social Life of Information*. Boston: Harvard Business School Press, 2000.

Seely Brown, John, Steve Denning, Katalina Groh, and Laurence Prusak. *Storytelling in Organizations*. Burlington: Elsevier Butterworth-Heinemann, 2005.

Senge, Peter. *The Fifth Discipline Fieldbook*. New York: Doubleday, 1994.

Sharma, Robin. *Leadership Wisdom from the Monk Who Sold His Ferrari*. Toronto: HarperCollins, 1998.

Siegel, M. A. "Falling Asleep at Your Keyboard: The Case for Computer Imagination." *Training Today, The Magazine of the American Society for Training and Development* (March/April 2003): 13–15.

Siegel, M. A. "The Future of Education," in *Catalog of Tomorrow: Trends Shaping Your Future,* A. Zolli, ed. Indianapolis: Que, 2003.

Siegel, M. A., and D. M. Davis. *Understanding Computer-Based Education*. New York: Random House, 1986.

Siegel, M. A., S. Ellis, and M. Lewis. "Deep Conversations: Designing for Deep Conversation in a Scenarios-based e-Learning Environment" (academic paper, 2003).

Simmons, Annette. *The Story Factor*. Cambridge: Perseus Publishing, 2001.

Slywotsky, Adrian. *The Art of Profitability*. New York: Warner Books, 2002.

Stone, Douglas, Bruce Patton, and Sheila Heen. *Difficult Conversations*. New York: Penguin, 1999.

Surowiecki, James. *The Wisdom of Crowds*. New York: Random House, 2004.

Tierno, Michael. *Aristotle's Poetics for Screenwriters*. New York: Hyperion, 2002.

Tolle, Eckhart. *The Power of Now*. Novato: New World Library, 1999.

van Adelsberg, David, and Edward Trolley. *Running Training Like a Business*. San Francisco: Berrett-Koehler Publishers, 1999.

Walker, Michael Chase. *Power Screenwriting*. Hollywood: Lone Eagle Publishing, 2002.

Watkins, Michael. *The First 90 Days*. Boston: Harvard Business School Press, 2003.

Whiteley, Richard, and Diane Hessan. *Customer Centered Growth*. Reading: Addison-Wesley, 1996.

Wineburg, Sam. *Historical Thinking and Other Unnatural Acts*. Philadelphia: Temple University Press, 2001.

Wurman, Richard Saul. *Understanding*. TED Conferences, Inc., 2000.

Wurman, Richard Saul. *Information Anxiety 2*. Indianapolis: Que, 2001.

Zander, Rosamund Stone, and Benjamin Zander. *The Art of Possibility*. New York: Penguin, 2000.

MY STORY MATRIX

Leadership Performance Skills

Me

Story Types

Story Types	Leadership Performance Skills				Me
Success					
Failure					
Fun					
Legends					

CPSIA information can be obtained at www.ICGtesting.com
Printed in the USA
LVOW110108151112

307375LV00001B/1/P